A HISTORY

OF THE

22nd (Service) Battalion

Royal Fusiliers

(KENSINGTON).

———

Edited by

Major Christopher Stone, D.S.O., M.C.

———

1923.

Privately Printed for the Old Comrades Association
of the Battalion.

HISTORY OF THE
22nd ROYAL FUSILIERS.

CONTENTS.

EDITOR'S NOTE.

This book has been compiled primarily not for the general public, nor even for the friends of the Battalion, but for the actual surviving members of the Battalion, in the hope that a connected account, however brief and fragmentary, may be of interest to them as a record, and that here and there a chance word or name may serve to light up for them those corridors and side-shows of memory in which even the most reticent of us love to wander. Fragmentary it is bound to be, and inaccurate too, by faults of omission as well as commission. Corrections and additions will occur to all readers, who are requested to communicate their suggestions to the Editor of *Mufti* for publication and for use in any future edition of the History.

It is unnecessary for me to say that Sir William Davison has been the motive force in this compilation and has supplied information, made suggestions, read the proofs, and helped the Committee to face the financial problem of publication. Nor has the Committee been behind-hand in giving me all the help and support that are required by the Editor of a book of this sort; for instance, by taking from my shoulders the responsibility of deciding that in Appendix I all decorations awarded subsequently to the disbandment of the Battalion should be omitted.

We are indebted to Mr. J. Bull for the beautiful design on the cover, which he originally made for *Mufti*: and to Mr. H. C. Waddams for the map at the end of the volume on which he has traced the intricate journeyings of the Battalion. The delay in publication caused by his offer to make this map when the rest of the book was already in the printer's hands, will be more than condoned by those who follow the itinerary of the Battalion through those unforgotten villages.

To these, to Mr. Rosewarne our indefatigable printer, and to others who have helped in the common endeavour to secure a coherent record from the salvage dumps, I offer my sincere thanks.

C. S.

February, 1923.

6

FOREWORD.

I have been asked to write a *Foreword* to a brief history of the formation and active service in France and Flanders during the Great War of the 22nd Battalion Royal Fusiliers (Kensington), which was raised by me in response to Lord Kitchener's appeal for men in September, 1914, and in order to explain how the raising of the Regiment came about it is necessary to say a few words as to the position in which the Royal Borough of Kensington, of which I was Mayor, found itself when war was declared.

The news of August 4th, 1914, that we were at war with Germany, though it came as a shock to the people of Kensington, as it did to people in other parts of the country, perhaps found them better prepared towards meeting the great emergency which had arisen than was generally the case elsewhere.

Curiously enough, some five months previously, in February and March, 1914, I had, as Mayor of Kensington, inaugurated an active recruiting campaign on behalf of our local Territorial Battalion, the 13th (Princess Louise's) Kensington Battalion of the London Regiment, whose numbers had fallen below what was adequate for efficient battalion training. I spoke at a number of large meetings, notably those at the Coronet Theatre, the Picture Palace, Portobello Road, and a Great Rally at the Battalion Drill Hall in Iverna Gardens, as the result of which a very considerable number of men were added to the strength of the Regiment.

Later in the year, between May 14th and 20th, 1914, a special National Reserve Week was held in Kensington under my presidency, to raise money to provide Headquarters for the Kensington Battalion of the National Reserve, which was much hampered for lack of equipment and accommodation. The " Globe " newspaper, in referring to this effort, remarked in an editorial that

" unfortunately it did not often happen in England that the civil authorities united with the military organisation to improve the national defences—this, however, would be seen in Kensington during the forthcoming National Reserve Week."

As a result of this Week, Headquarters, with miniature rifle shooting range, were obtained at 102, Ladbroke Grove, North Kensington, in which accommodation was found for the National Reserve Battalion, which was then raised to a strength of some 70 officers and 500 men, all of whom had previously served in the Forces of the Crown.

Though unforeseen at the time, this event proved of great importance in connection with the early training of the 22nd Royal Fusiliers, and the provision of its original quota of officers.

Another curious coincidence, in view of coming events, was the fact that on the 23rd May, 1914, we arranged for a general mobilisation as far as possible under war conditions of the eight Detachments of our local Division of the British Red Cross Society, which had been inaugurated in 1910 during the Mayoralty of one of my predecessors, Sir Walter (now Lord) Phillimore. The War Office appointed special officers to inspect and report, and a scheme of operation was drawn up, based on the assumption that severe fighting had been taking place in the Home Counties, and that the Kensington Division had been warned of casualties arriving by road and rail, in preparation for which an Ambulance Train and Rest Station were to be prepared at Addison Road Station, and an Isolation Hospital in an empty house in Lexham Gardens. Kensington Town Hall, under the scheme, became a General Hospital, while a temporary Hospital was provided at the Vicarage Hall, with medical and surgical wards.

In these ways the citizens of Kensington had endeavoured to prepare themselves as far as possible to meet the dread calamity of war, should it ever come to pass.

The period of waiting was not long.

On Tuesday, August 4th, the day after the August Bank Holiday, war with Germany was declared.

Immediate arrangements were made for the mobilisation of the 13th Kensingtons. I opened a Recruiting Office at the Town Hall, and in a few days the Regiment was raised to its full complement of about 1,100 men. The Town Hall kitchens were temporarily used as a cookhouse for the Battalion, some 3,000 meals being daily provided there. The Kensington Red Cross also temporarily established local Headquarters at the Town Hall, and medical and surgical stores and blankets, of which there was found to be a deficiency at Headquarters, began to pour in, in response to an appeal which had been issued.

On Sunday, August 9th, the 13th Kensingtons, now at full strength, after a drum-head service in Kensington Gardens, handed me their Colours for safe keeping at the Town Hall, and marched out of London preparatory to their embarkation a few weeks later for France.

Leave was then given by the War Office for the immediate recruitment of a second Battalion of this Regiment, and once more recruiting was started at the Town Hall. As soon as the Recruiting Office had been opened, so great was the rush of the young men of the district who were anxious to join, that it was necessary to form them into a queue, which extended during the greater part of the first day from the Town Hall beyond the entrance of St. Mary Abbot's Church. Under these circumstances only a few days were necessary to complete the recruitment of this second Battalion of the 13th to full strength, and they in turn left London to undergo a course of training.

The two Battalions asked for by the War Office from our local Territorial Regiment having thus been raised, and there being still a large number of young men in Kensington for whom places in these Battalions could not be found, I went to the War Office and expressed my willingness to accept the responsibility of raising and equipping a Service Battalion for the " New Army," in response to the urgent appeal for more men which had just been made by Lord Kitchener.

Unfortunately, considerable delay occurred before the authorities at the War Office finally decided to accept my offer, and it was not until the 9th September that sanction was finally granted me to proceed. By reason of this delay on the part of the War Office large numbers of the young men in the business houses in Kensington, who had signified their desire to join a local Service Battalion, had enlisted in other regiments. It was consequently necessary once more to start recruiting, both at the Town Hall and at the National Reserve Headquarters in North Kensington.

In connection with the recruiting of the 22nd R.F., a special poster, showing a wounded British soldier who had just disposed of three Uhlans, was designed by Mr. John Hassall, R.I., with the title : " It's 4 to 1—come and help us lads, quick." I showed this poster to Lord Kitchener at his request, and he greatly admired it, but criticised the fact that the breeches of one of the wounded

9

Uhlans were too smart. "No Uhlan," said Lord Kitchener, "ever had decently cut breeches." I informed Mr. Hassall of this criticism, and several deep creases were accordingly inserted in the offending breeches. The poster was then finally approved by Lord Kitchener.

After some six hundred men had been enrolled, I was informed by Major-General Sir Francis Lloyd, K.C.B., etc., who was the G.O.C. London District, that a body of Colonials, some hundreds strong, who had patriotically crossed the seas in order to offer their services to the Mother Country in her hour of need, and were anxious, if possible, to serve together in the same Battalion, were encamped in the White City, on the outskirts of Kensington. Sir Francis asked whether it would be possible for me to include these men in the new Kensington Battalion. To this I readily agreed, and the inclusion of these fine recruits from overseas undoubtedly did much to secure the splendid fighting qualities for which the Regiment became renowned after its arrival in France, where they went practically direct into the firing line.

The historian of " The Royal Fusiliers in the Great War " (Major H. C. O'Neill), writing of the 22nd R.F., says :—" The Battalion combined a very good type of Londoner and a very good type of Colonial, and the two amalgamated very successfully . . . earning for themselves a name for courageous and skilful fighting."

It was also the proud boast of their beloved Commanding Officer (Colonel Barnett Barker, D.S.O.), who took them overseas, that " the 22nd Battalion never lost a yard of trench or failed their comrades in the day of battle : such is your record, and such a record of you will be handed down to posterity."

I am, however, digressing from my narrative of the preliminaries connected with the raising of the Battalion.

Having secured the requisite number of men, I was next responsible, in accordance with the undertaking I had given to the War Office, for their training and equipment.

The National Reserve, to which I alluded above, not only furnished 250 men who had previously served the Crown, but also provided a nucleus of 16 officers, as well as the Regimental Sergeant-Major, in the person of Sergt.-Major (afterwards Captain) L. C. McCausland, who rendered most valuable services in the preliminary training of the Battalion.

I had then to appoint a Commanding Officer, and on the introduction of one of my Aldermen, Colonel (afterwards Major-General) W. F. Cavaye, I appointed Major J. A. Innes, late of the Rifle Brigade, who had been awarded a D.S.O. for his services with that regiment in the South African War. Colonel Innes, as he then became, commanded the Battalion during the greater part of its period of training, and gave me most valuable assistance in connection with its equipment, billeting, and hutting.

I was also exceptionally fortunate in securing shortly after this as Second in Command the services of Captain Randle Barnett Barker, late of the Welch Fusiliers, a relative by marriage of my wife, whose remarkable aptitude for training men in the art of war is well known to all members of the Battalion.

On the transfer of Colonel Innes by the War Office to the Command of the Reserve Battalion (the 27th Royal Fusiliers), Major Barnett Barker assumed the Command of the 22nd, and it was under him that the Regiment went overseas and fought most of their hardest fights. No regiment could have had a better commanding officer; he knew every man in the Battalion, and was loved and trusted by all ranks.

After providing officers for the preliminary training of the Battalion, and later securing young officers in place of some of the National Reserve officers whose age precluded them from going with the Battalion overseas, the next urgent matter was that of equipment, for which, as I said, the War Office held me responsible, though unable to provide any assistance except by giving me a list of Government Contractors, all of whom I found were already fully engaged with Government orders for more than a year ahead. I accordingly turned to various Kensington firms to assist me in my difficulty, and was able to purchase through Sir Richard Burbidge, Bart., the Managing Director of Harrod's, some of the last khaki obtainable in London, with which the Battalion was clothed while most of the Government-raised regiments were still in " workhouse blue."

With regard to the military equipment, through the kindness of Sir Francis Lloyd, whose helpful advice throughout was invaluable to me, I obtained patterns from Woolwich, and eventually induced Messrs. Lillywhite, the cricket outfitters, to undertake the job, as I found that they had stores of excellent leather intended for cricket bags and other like purposes. The equipment when completed was pronounced by the War Office authorities to be in every way first class, both in material and workmanship, and Messrs. Lillywhite subsequently received orders for many thousand sets from the Government.

Among minor matters of equipment I was unwittingly assisted by the great German firm of Kropp, as I was able to purchase from

Messrs. Derry and Toms, of Kensington, 1,100 of the best quality hollow ground Kropp razors at a reasonable figure. This purchase, I believe, added considerably to the comfort of the men and to the smartness of their appearance, both during their training and afterwards when at the front. Derry and Toms also supplied me with excellent khaki shirts, which were much appreciated at a time when such things were difficult to obtain except by officers at very high prices.

Provision having been made in respect of officers and equipment, the next responsibility which faced me was the provision of a suitable Camp and Training Ground for the Battalion, as I formed the opinion that the accommodation provided in the White City, which had been hired by the Government from Mr. Imre Kiralfy, was highly unsatisfactory, and I was also not prepared to enter into the very onerous contract which Mr. Kiralfy demanded from all those who used his premises. I accordingly arranged with Colonel Innes, whose home was at Horsham, in Sussex, to hire land from him at the village of Roffey, about two miles from the town of Horsham, on which I erected a camp on plans approved by the War Office, but considerably improved by the Architect whom I employed, Mr. Frederick Wheeler, F.R.I.B.A., of 7, Stone Buildings, Lincoln's Inn.

Having made up my mind that the White City was unsuitable as winter quarters for the Battalion, I communicated this decision to Sir Francis Lloyd. His reply was that if I took the men out of London they must be removed at once. I informed him that I could not remove them that week, as it was then Friday afternoon, but that I would have them away before noon on the following Tuesday. Officers were at once sent to Horsham to arrange for the billeting of the Battalion until such time as the Camp was completed, and at 10.15 a.m. on the morning of Tuesday, the 27th October, 1914, the Battalion entrained in two long special trains at Addison Road Station for their new home in Sussex.

Having got the men and the officers, and having clothed them and equipped them, and having obtained land for a camp and signed the contract with a firm of builders for the erection of hutments, I began to think my work was nearly completed, but I had overlooked the vast equipment which had to be provided under War Office regulations for the camp of an infantry battalion.

A schedule of 10 closely printed pages reached me from the War Office, requiring me to provide in the course of a few weeks every kind of household requisite needed for a camp of 1,100 men, and this at a time when the Government had already bought up all available stocks. I had to provide beds, bolster-cases, palliasses, chairs, knives, forks, basins, brushes, tubs, mops, shovels, kitchen utensils—trivets, ladles, baking-dishes, skimmers—equipment for Ablution Rooms, for Drying Rooms, for Guard Rooms, for Orderly Rooms, for sanitary offices, for Quartermaster's Stores, for Quartermaster's Offices, for Officers' Mess, for coal yard, as well as barrows, shovels, weighing machines, etc., etc., and a Recreation establishment with backgammon, chess, dominoes, draughts and solitaire. I cannot trace in my accounts any record of the purchase of sets of solitaire, but I believe most of the other things came along sooner or later. Some of the things I got through the War Office, others I purchased as and when I could. I had a fierce tussle with the War Office to allow me to supply iron bedsteads with spring mattresses, which were contrary to regulations, but I eventually had my way, and I believe these beds added materially to the comfort of the men while they were in camp.

I must not leave the matter of equipment without acknowledging my great indebtedness to the ability and tireless industry of my private secretary, Mr. G. A. Hames, who, much to his regret, had been rejected for military service. His powers of obtaining comparative estimates and of arranging and testing samples so as to secure the best value, were of the greatest service to myself and to the Battalion.

Little remains for me to tell with regard to the initial stages of the making of a very gallant regiment. Early in March, 1915, the men left their billets in Horsham, where they had been treated with the greatest kindness and hospitality, and took up their quarters in the new camp, which, though possibly not so comfortable as the old billets, was much better suited for training purposes and for fitting the men for the great adventure overseas for which they had volunteered, and on which they were impatient to commence.

An important item in camp life is the provision of good and well-cooked food, and I am glad to say that Major Barker, who was then Second in Command, and as such was largely responsible for the catering, felt on this matter as I did. We were also fortunate in having in the person of Seigt. Cook Fowles a man who in the kitchen of the Great Central Hotel had acquired great experience in the preparation of food. Lord Kitchener was much interested in an ordinary week's specimen menu which I sent to him, having regard to the complaints which were then being received by the War Office from many training camps as to the insufficiency and monotony of the food provided. I don't think we ever had a serious complaint in either of these respects all the time the Regiment was under my care at Roffey, though I was spending many thousands of pounds a year less than the amount I could have demanded from the War Office for the feeding of the men.

On the 1st July, 1915, my responsibility for the Battalion came to an end. On that date I handed it, with its equipment, and the camp, over to the War Office, and in acknowledgment I received the following letter of thanks from the Army Council :—

"Sir,—I am commanded by the Army Council to offer you their sincere thanks for having raised the 22nd (Service) Battalion Royal Fusiliers (Kensington), of which the administration has now been taken over by the military authorities. The Council much appreciate the spirit which prompted your offer of assistance, and they are gratified at the successful results of the time and labour devoted to this object, which has added to the armed forces of the Crown the services of a fine body of men. The Army Council will watch the future career of the battalion with interest, and they feel assured that when sent to the front it will maintain the high reputation of the distinguished regiment of which it forms part. I am to add that its success on active service will largely depend on the result of your efforts to keep the depôt companies constantly up to establishment with men in every way fit for service in the field.

                              I am, Sir,
                                   Your obedient servant,
                                        (signed) B. B. CUBITT."

Though my responsibility had ceased, my undertaking to the War Office having been discharged, I need scarcely say that my interest in the Battalion and in the welfare of its officers, non-commissioned officers and men was as great as ever. I kept a roll of all ranks at the Town Hall, and arranged with Colonel Barker, who had then assumed the Command of the Battalion, to keep me fully informed of every casualty, so that I might at once communicate with the next of kin. During the two years in which he commanded the Battalion on active service, until he was made a Brigadier-General, he wrote me over 160 letters. No matter affecting a man in the Battalion or his family at home in which he thought I might be able to help was too small or trivial for him to write about, as he looked on the Regiment as his family. At the same time, no matter which affected the Battalion was too big for him to write to me to go to the War Office to have it altered and put right. He had an exaggerated idea of my powers over the military hierarchy, by reason of my success in getting a move on in certain matters with which he was personally acquainted. Often, wearied out after a heavy day's fighting, he would not go to sleep without sending me the list of the casualities of the day, so that their relatives might know as soon as possible, and without waiting for the often misleading and generally delayed official communication. Many were the letters of thanks I received from relatives to whom I had sent on the Colonel's message about someone they loved dearly.

Few who heard or have read them are likely to forget the stirring words with which he, as General in Command of the 99th Brigade, addressed the 22nd on their disbandment, when, owing to lack of men, Brigades were reduced from four to three Battalions, and the lot fell on the 22nd to be disbanded. They are quoted at length by the historian of " The Royal Fusiliers in the Great War," and will be found later in this volume. More than to anyone else the Battalion owes gratitude and affectionate remembrance to this gallant and lovable man, who died, as he would have wished, a soldier's death.

WILLIAM H. DAVISON.

CHAPTER I.

THE BEGINNING.

By J. M. GREENSLADE, M.M.

" You (name) are required to attend at ten o'clock a.m. on the 28th day of September, 1914, at Shepherd's Bush (White City) for the purpose of appearing before a Justice to be attested for His Majesty's Army, in which you have expressed your willingness to serve."

The blue paper which bore this injunction was our introduction to the 22nd (Kensington) Battalion, Royal Fusiliers, as it subsequently was called. At the moment it was merely an attestation form, and we had no unit officially, although we were being sworn in at the Town Hall, Kensington, for a new battalion of Kitchener's Army at the invitation of the Mayor of Kensington (Alderman W. H. Davison). Major Barnett Barker was there, and there was a queue as for a matinee.

At the same time recruiting was taking place, we understood, at the Polytechnic in Regent Street, and we all met on the fateful 28th at the White City, as enjoined by our notice in the space marked " here name some place." It was *some* place with a vengeance.

Amid the fading and shabby glories of " marble " palaces, in surroundings in which many of us had enjoyed rollicking evenings in Venetian or Japanese imaginings, we formed up shoulder to shoulder in platoons and companies. Many of us had popped a toothbrush and razor in our waistcoat pockets, and perhaps a clean collar for emergencies. We might be in prison or in France that night, for all we knew. But it was reassuring to see Sir (as he now is) William Davison there, chatting with us and helping Major Barnett Barker to sort us out.

How they found out which were N.C.O.'s and which were privates was a miracle. Memory will have it that each man was asked whether he had ever been (*a*) a soldier before; (*b*) a boy scout; (*c*) in uniform of any description. Then memory further deponeth that as names were called in alphabetical order, so we took

16

our position, and that by quartering each platoon and nominating the right hand man of each section, four N.C.O.'s were found supplementary to those who had had any kind of drill before.

Behold us then in companies, platoons and sections—many of us mated for eventful years, which afterwards scattered us, mowed some of us down, bound others together by association in the biggest war in history, and made us all on the spot fellow-soldiers instead of a mere bunch of civilians, laughing and sneering at what seemed to be the red tape of the proceedings.

We had joined for three years with the Colours, with the proviso " or the duration of the war if such is longer than three years." It would be invidious and unnecessary to recall names that occur to the mind as one visualises that parade. We were all respectably dressed, as someone commented—it was a gathering of the cuffs and collar brigade.

And as we stood patiently enduring the shuffling of the numbers and the pinning on of temporary badges, and so on, we had a glimpse of swarthy, strenuous, shirted men marching past in rhythmic step and with faces set. It was just what we wanted to make us realise that that was how we should be presently—human automata to be moved at the will of one man.

They were the Colonials, and we were destined to " soldier " with them. They were to be our A and B companies. We were C and D, and if there was any friction in the amalgamation of the two half-battalions, it was short lived. But friendly rivalry in efficiency survived for a long time, and if the Colonials, as we called them, resented Londoners being foisted upon them, we understood their temper and learned to be proud to be in " their " battalion, as they called it.

The question of " theirs " or " ours " came to a head very soon, when our first C.O., Lieut.-Col. J. A. Innes, D.S.O., put it bluntly to all four companies on parade on Wormwood Scrubs. Did we wish to be known as the Colonial battalion or as the Kensington battalion?

Two companies naturally voted one way and two another, but the Colonel seized on the report of the D Company officer that his men did not care a damn what they were called so long as they went to France, and he praised that spirit, and announced that we were the Kensington Battalion. Which was probably just as well. Anyhow, we knew each other for a long time as " Colonials " and " Kensingtons," until we had got mixed up a bit.

17

There was not room at the White City for all of us to billet " in," so some of us journeyed to and fro each day between our homes and our parade ground.

Regtl. Sergt.-Major McCausland was a most affrighting figure to us, and we soon learned that being late at the office or at business was nothing compared to failing to be in readiness for parade *before* the time appointed each morning. Those preliminary exercises on Wormwood Scrubs made all of us stiff for days, but we enjoyed them. We felt the effect, and when we were issued with broom handles for sentry-go we did not think that after all it was so very funny.

Then there was the issue of boots, which were very welcome, as the manœuvres on the dusty Scrubs became more elaborate and intensive. They were exhilarating days, and we seemed to have been there ages when rumours of a move came round. It had been a change to parade occasionally in Kensington Gardens, where the officers' language made the nurse girls giggle. But everyone was soon sick of the White City, especially those billeted there, and the subsequent scandal of the feeding of the troops brought the contractors under public notice.

Then came the eventful day when we marched through Bayswater and Oxford Street in all the pride of our young soldierhood to fetch our antiquated rifles from the Tower, and the excitement of the return journey *via* Piccadilly in the rain. There was the anti-climax of cleaning the cursed weapons, and the comforting reflection that, after all, two men had to share each gun.

Rumour quickly named our destination—Horsham—and after we had been at the White City barely a month, during which we had been praised by General Sir Francis Lloyd, we bade London a fond farewell, and marched through cheering crowds to Addison Road Station. If we had been going to France we should not have been more touched by the demonstrative send-off we had. We had grown in number considerably during the few weeks, and must have been 1,000 strong at Horsham. By the time we had reached that hospitable town, in which we sojourned so happily, we had decided on our partners for our billets.

On arrival, we were paraded in the Roffey road, and partnered off for billets. A, B, and C companies were marched into Horsham, and D company found themselves at Roffey, a village a couple of miles from the town.

18

It was nearly Christmas before the battalion had completely shed its mufti, but by degrees the khaki predominated, and the sight of N.C.O.'s or men in khaki tunics and bowler hats became extremely rare. We rapidly acquired steadiness in the ranks, proficiency in drill, and accuracy in handling our heavy rifles, to which the short bayonet had to be fixed (in sheath). There were manœuvres on Plummer's Plain and Manning's Heath, and encores once or twice when Mrs. Innes found pleasure in our achievements. She was assiduous in watching our development, and generally drove with us on our route marches.

In the early spring the huts that had been in course of erection at Roffey for our accommodation were completed, and, in March, when Christmas and New Year leaves had become a memory, we took down our khaki caps from their nails in our billets, consoled ourselves with the thought that we should not be far from our kind hosts and hostesses, and marched into the neatest and most comfortable camp we were ever destined to occupy.

We were a little colony all to ourselves, and we soon took pride in the correct arrangement of kit for inspections and in the visits of admiring lady friends to see us peeling the " spuds " on Sundays. The hut orderlies became more and more proficient, and in a month or two the little red permanent passes made their appearance. It allowed the owner to be absent from his quarters from retreat until 12 midnight, except when on duty. Unfortunately, C.B. or " crime " made it forfeit, and woe betide the delinquent who could not answer his name when the orderly sergeant made his final round.

It was inevitable, of course, that a talented battalion such as ours should not exist long away from home without having its own journal. Major Christopher Stone, then Lieutenant O.C. Signals, and Lieutenant Murray, were active in putting our first " rag " on the stocks, and it was launched on February 15th, 1915, under the title " 22nd Battalion Royal Fusiliers' Fortnightly Gazette." It was in the form of a four-page folder, and was sold at 1d.

It opened with an introduction by Lieutenant Murray, and there was a delightful reminder of our old friend Fraser in a column on bayonet fighting. Trench digging was also commented on, and Frank Gee, the irrepressible, sang about " The Inoculation "—a delicate little attention on the part of the M.O. which occasioned more dismay, in anticipation, than the most grilling experience in France.

A writer, named "Bottlenose," described an exciting draw in the Cup Final match between A Company and C Company, and "J.W." asked several pertinent questions, such as "When are we going to the front?" and "If the slippers were really served out for the men to double round the Pyramids in Egypt?" Corporal C. A. Downs commenced a valuable series of articles on physical training, and Sergeant M. van Jaarsveld revealed himself as editor, *pro tem.*

The fact that R.S.M. McCausland was becoming Lieutenant in the C Company was announced, and that R.S.M. Dunlop was succeeding him as R.S.M. There was a reference to a B Company dance at the Black Horse Hotel, arranged by Sergt. A. E. Hughes, with Sergt.-Major Rossell as M.C. and Lance-Corpl. Leonard, Ptes. Gurney, Markie, M. Plummer and Wharton as stewards.

The next number (March 1st) was a much more ambitious production, with cover, and carrying several advertisements. The Editor acknowledged the help of Pte. Archie McKeen. Pte. P. Cannot (B.5) came on the scene with his capital cartoons, and there was a parting salute to Major Chance, who said "goodbye" to A Company on taking over a command in the British Empire League Ammunition Column (R.F.A.).

A Company won the cup presented by Father Cassidy, thanks to Manuel scoring in the replay against C Company. The trophy was presented by the Mayoress of Kensington. The teams were :—A Company : Emerson, Davis, O'Donnell, Hand, Jones, Holliday, Fraery, Wratten, Manuel, Webb, and Hayward. C Company : Hearn, Werman, Miles, Kennedy, Elliot, Coyland, Prince, Shankster, Robinson, Williams, and Everett.

Teddy Rutland gave us that stirring march song, "Are we downhearted?" and the answer is "No, no, no." The following Rugger team beat the 6th City of London Rifle Brigade :—Lieut. Woods, Bailey, Addison, Beyers, Sergt. Hughes; Lieut. Grant and Corpl. Downs; Brunton (Captain), Lieut. Smith, Sergeant Van Jaarsveld, Avila, Lieut. Walsh, Lance-Corpl. Barcham, Gifford, and Reece. Lance-Corpl. Johnnie Walker appeared as a comedian at the Electric Theatre.

Before the third number was published on March 15th, the Battalion were in huts. The Battalion had been inspected on the 6th by Major-General Drummond, M.V.O., accompanied by Brigadier-General Twigg, Lieut.-Colonel Innes, D.S.O., and Major Barker. The Mayor of Kensington was also present.

There was a successful concert given in the Carfax Theatre by Teddy Rutland. Among those who pushed the programme along were Corpl. Abbey, Pte. Stapley, C.Q.M.S. Hurt, Pte. Markie, and Sgt.In.Mus. Burgess.

Further talent in the concert line was revealed at the Y.M.C.A. concert later. Names recorded are Sergt. Heffill, Pte. Spear, Pte. Jackson, Pte. Jack Jones, Corpl. Upton, Sergt. Saunders, Pte. Wilson, Pte. Sexton, Pte. Archer, and Pte. Blackburn.

The first cross-country run was held on March 17th, when Pte. Dickson (D) beat Pte. Britton (D) by a few yards in an exciting five miles chase.

Captain Clifford went from B to A during March. A team representing the Battalion played the Horsham Golf Club, and were defeated by seven matches to two, with one halved. Our team was:—Pte. Lewis, Lieut. Woods, Pte. Woods, Pte. Stuart. Pte. Dennis, Lance-Corpl. Pignon, Pte. A. Hennessy, Pte. Gee, Pte. Hennessy, and Pte. Palmer.

In April Frank Gee became Assistant Editor of the "Fortnightly Gazette." Pte. F. P. Soar (C) was Sales and Business Manager. A bit of excitement was occasioned by a Zeppelin scare parade. At 11 p.m. we turned out in full drill order, with an issue of ball cartridges. The Zepp did not come nearer than Norfolk.

Major Wilkieson (C) went to Hythe for a course in musketry. The Adjutant (Lieut. Phythian Adams) presented six bugles to the band. The Battalian football team won the Horsham Charity Cup —an exciting match with Horsham County. Jock Martin was the captain, and the goals were scored by Robinson (2) and Brown (1). A demonstration on the field by 13 Platoon in a weird array of blankets brought money to Horsham charities.

Excerpts from Battalion Orders include :—Dress 347, officers' marching order : Haversack, water bottle, field glasses or telescope, pocket book A.B.153, compass, great coat or waterproof sheet, Para. 1711 K.R. drill order: Sam Browne belt without sword frog.

N.C.O.'s and men :—Marching order : Haversack, water bottle, entrenching tool, and pack containing the following articles : Cap comforter, hold-all containing one pair laces, tooth brush, razor and case, shaving brush and comb, great coat, housewife (fitted), mess tin and cover, and socks (worsted) one pair; soap, one piece; towel, one. Drill order : Belt with side arms, walking out belt and swagger cane.

Pte. John Braden, aged 42, of A Company, died in April, and was given a military funeral. Officers of the battalion sent a beautiful wreath on the occasion of the funeral of Mrs. James Innes, mother of the Commanding Officer.

A miniature rifle range was opened in the camp by Mrs. Innes, who scored a " bull." There was a match between officers and sergeants on May 6th; sergeants 489, officers 486. The winning team consisted of C.S.M. Rossell, Sergt. Kerry, C.Q.M.S. Symonds, Sergt. Saunders, C.Q.M.S. Stacpoole, C.S.M. Smith, Sergts. Hartley, Drew Gardner, C.S.M. Kidd, Sergt. Neave, and R.S.M. Dunlop—in the order of their score. Officers were :— Lieuts. Grant and Lambert, Major Boardman, Capt. Daman, Lieuts. Evans and Thompson, Major Powlett, Lieuts. B. Woods, Hooke, Moore, Roscoe, and Godlonton.

B Company sports were held on May 12th, and the Battalion sports took place on the 26th at Roffey. A creditable souvenir programme was printed for the occasion, and the special sports number of the " Gazette " appeared on June 7th.

In it was a column devoted to Sergt. Rogers and the Provost Staff (Regimental police) and a picture of the orderly room staff. This was, of course, incidental.

There were excellent photographs, and Corpl. Pignon recorded that the sports meeting was a tremendous success. Mrs. Davison, the Mayoress of Kensington, presented the prizes, as follows :—

100 Yards—Pte. W. J. Gray, B, 1 ; Pte. A. W. Britton, D, 2 ; C.-S.-M. Rossell, B, 3 ; Lieut. Lambert, B, 4. Time, 10 3/5 secs.

220 Yards—Pte. Britton D and Pte. Gray B, dead heat; Pte. Prince, C, 3 ; L.-Corpl. Evenett, C, 4. Time, 24 3/5 secs.

440 Yards—Pte. Britton, D, 1 ; Pte. Gray B, 2 ; L.-Corpl. Turner, A, 3 ; Lieut. Evans, D, 4, Time, 59 1/5 secs.

880 Yards—Pte. Britton, D, 1 ; L.-Corpl. Turner, A, 2 ; Pte. Jones, A, 3 ; Pte. Newman, B, 4. Time, 2 mins. 1 secs.

One Mile—Pte. J. C. Dixon, D, 1; L.-Corpl. Turner, A, 2 ; Pte. Jones, A, 3 ; Lieut. Grant, A, 4. Time, 5 mins. 12 1/5 secs.

Inter-Company Team (Three Miles)—Pte. Dixon, D, 1 ; Pte. Forman, D, 2 ; Pte. Bedford, D, 3 ; L.-Corpl. Wenman, C, 4. Time, 15 mins. 11 secs.

120 Yards Hurdles—C.-S.-M. Rossell, B, 1 ; Pte. Neyland, B, 2 ; Lieut. Walsh, B, 3.

Inter-Company Relay (One Mile)—Winners, D Company — 880, Pte. Dixon ; 440, Pte. Britton ; 220, Lieut. Evans and Pte. Ward.

Officers *v* Sergeants—Officers won.

Putting the Shot—C.-S.-M. Rossell, B, 32 ft. 2 in., 1 ; Lieut. Walsh, B, 29 ft. 4 in., 2 ; Pte. O'Donnell, A, 28 ft. 2 in., 3.

High Jump—C.-S.-M. Rossell, B, 5 ft. 2 in., 1 ; Lieut. Walsh, B, 5 ft. 1 in., 2 ; Pte. Spear, D, 5 ft., 3.

Long Jump—C.-S.-M. Rossell, B, 19 ft. 6 in., 1 ; Lieut. Walsh, B, 2 ; Pte. Prince, C, 3.

Throwing Cricket Ball—Pte. Judge, C, 102 yds., 1 ; Lieut. Evans, D, 88 yds., 2 ; Lieut. Woods, 85 yds., 6 ins., 3.

Inter-Company Tug-of-War (Final)—B Company beat C Company, two pulls to one.

Bayonet Fighting (Final)—Pte. Brown, D, beat Pte. Taylor, B, three points to one.

Boot Melee—Pte. A. Smith, C, 1 ; Pte. Gardner, B, 2 ; Pte. Watson, C, 3 ; Pte. McWilliam, D, 4.

Band Race—L.-Corpl. Whibley, 1 ; Pte. Woodley, 2 ; Pte. Watson, 3 ; Pte. Griffin, 4.

Pillow Fight—L.-Corpl. North, 1 ; Pte. King, 2 ; Pte. Brown, 3.

The C.O. and Mrs. Innes received the congratulations of the Battalion in June, on the birth of a young Fusilier.

Brigadier-General Kellett, from the Royal Irish Regiment, became known to the Battalion as the Brigadier. The strength of the Battalion had been considerably increased through the recruiting efforts of Sergt. Kerfoot (in Manchester) and Sergt. Hartley (in London), and Sergt.-Major Hurt was put in charge of a newly-formed E Company, under Captain Colvile.

Just when the sweet peas were coming on nicely we had notice to quit our comfortable huts and pack up for Clipstone, and a souvenir number of the " Gazette " was published on June 26th.

Lots of people won't believe we had sherry trifle at Roffey. Before we leave it let us note that fact. Thirty bottles of sherry were used for it. Our diet sheet was a monument to the zeal of Major Barnett-Barker. Here is a sample of the menu, which was called " Diet sheet " in those days :—

Thursday.—Breakfast : Porridge, one fried egg and bacon, bread and marmalade, tea and coffee. Dinner : Vegetable soup, boiled beef, greens, dumplings, potatoes, mixed fruits and pudding. Tea : Tea, cake, bread and butter. Supper : Soup, corned beef, bread and butter. Full ration of bread to be drawn on this day.

Friday.—Breakfast : Porridge, liver and bacon, bread and butter, tea and coffee. Dinner : Lentil soup, roast mutton, onion sauce, potatoes, stewed gooseberries and custard. Tea : Tea, watercress and spring onions, bread and butter.

Saturday.—Breakfast : Porridge; half company, steak and onions, chipped potatoes; half company, one fried egg and bacon; bread and marmalade, tea and coffee. Dinner : Pea soup, roast beef, Yorkshire pudding, potatoes, plum pudding and white sauce. Tea : Tea, jam, bread and butter.

Sergt. Fowles was in charge of the cookhouse.

At the end of June we bade a fond farewell to Horsham. Entraining at an unearthly hour, we must have tested the devotion of the good citizens, who were awakened by the cheering, and the band, and the laughter. It was a merry send-off we had. All Horsham was there, and the laughter changed to tears in not a few cases as we were taken and the girls were left.

We travelled direct to Peterborough, and had beer and sandwiches there on the station. Then on to Edwinstowe, and marched past the Dukeries Hotel (how resolute had discipline made us !) to Clipstone.

During our month's sojourn in that dreary waste of huts, three miles from Mansfield, but conveniently near Nottingham at weekends, we thought we were roughing it. Well, we were; but during the next few years even Clipstone would not have been the least pleasant of our resting places. Notwithstanding the transplanting, the " Gazette " still bloomed. On July 19th it said :—

"We should like to express, in this first Clipstone number, a word of greeting to all those who with us form the 33rd Infantry Division. The Royal Fusiliers are particularly strong, there being no less than eight Battalions of our Regiment here, and when the time comes to show the stuff we are made of, the common badge and the same great regimental traditions which we share, will promote a feeling of solidity and *esprit de corps* that should stand us in excellent stead. Three Battalions of the Middlesex Regiment are also here. Their sub-title, " The Diehards," which the Regiment so richly earned at Albuhera, is a fair criterion of their quality. The 16th King's Royal Rifles is also part of the Division. Their rifle drill, which is at once a privilege and a distinction, carries with it all the honours and traditions of a glorious past. Finally, the 13th Battalion of the Essex Regiment, with its tradition of superb defence at Gibraltar and a long roll of later distinctions, completes our infantry establishment. The Army Service Corps is well represented and has, under very trying circumstances, served us splendidly."

[The eight R.F. Battalions were composed of the 17th (Empire), 18th, 19th 20th and 21st (Public Schools), 22nd (Kensington), 23rd and 24th (Sportsmen).]

The road between Mansfield and Clipstone became a veritable Brooklands track, and, unhappily, Corpl. J. H. Richardson, of C Company, was killed in the whirl of motor traffic. He was buried with full military honours.

We had barely got used to the new camp, trimmed it up, planted it, watered it, and acquired a taste for the flavour of coal dust, when once again we packed up. The whole Division was ordered to Salisbury Plain.

We had had a month at Clipstone, and we were not sorry to leave it. But the Plain! We stuck our chests out and realised that this was serious business.

The usual early morning start and the usual long day in a stuffy train. The monotony was, however, broken by the demonstrations at the junctions. They made us feel that we were going to fight for a country that appreciated our desire to serve.

Tidworth proved to be our destination this time. Half the Battalion was housed in palatial but overcrowded barracks. The other half had to use the tents. They had two drawbacks. It rained until we nearly became amphibious; and the earwigs often came in out of the wet.

August to November was spent at Tidworth, with the exception of an occasional night in a turnip field on long manœuvres over the countryside or in the trenches we had dug on the Plain. We were photographed and had our hair severely bobbed, and went as often as we could to London for week-ends, despite the two or three hours' crawl between Clapham Junction and Waterloo.

Our meals were as good as circumstances would permit, but the canteen was better. Everything was overworked and overcrowded. It was a relief to the soaked tenters when they were allowed to go into barracks instead of the other half battalion, but soon came the final farewell to England.

We had the review by Queen Mary, received our overseas kit, and having been overcharged by everybody who sold anything, we were the victims of spoilation by our Cavalry neighbours, who made it a pastime to secure any souvenirs they could from the chaps who were going across.

There was no time for anyone to be annoyed, because naturally we were away early in the morning, with Lord Kitchener's tract in our new active service pay book, which, by the way, made most of us, unaccountably, in debt.

Colonel Innes handed over the reins to Major Barnett Barker, who had made a brief tour of the trenches. He gave a lecture on what we might expect, and incidentally said anyone who cleaned his buttons out there would be shot at dawn.

Some of our men remained behind on munitions. Those who were bound on the great adventure and had had four days' special leave, looked eagerly forward to the march to Berlin.

As an indication of the spirits in which we spent the last few weeks at Tidworth, the following menu of a farewell dinner in the sergeants' mess—" a h...... of a mess too "—on September 29th, 1915, may well close this chapter. Here it is :—

MENU.

Soup.

Tomato, Bean Soup; Soup that never has bean soup ; and
Bean Soup that made Jack and the beans-talk.

Fish.

Fresh Salmon and Stale Gluckstein
White Sauce (p'raps).

Grand Entree.

Mutton Cutlets (on crutches)
Mashed Potatoes (for safety).
Mushroom Sauce (not mush-room for this).

Poultry (getting the " bird ").

Roast "Fowles" (with Dunlop rubber fittings).
French Beans (the saucy Cat).   Green Peas (ditto).

Joint.

Roast Beef (nice and juicy).   Veg. Marrow (no comments).
Baked Potatoes.   Horseradish Sauce (fresh from the horse).

Sweets (pet name for Sergeants).

Plum Pie ! D.S.O. (D—Soon Outed).
Custard (R.S.M. Dunlop did).
Blanc Mange (to strike matches on). Jellies (shake'em up Sergt.-Maj.)
Coffee.   Biscuits.   Cheese (from the mouse trap).
Stretcher Bearers in attendance afterwards.

———

The King may join us at Supper—
God Save the King.

═══════════

CHAPTER II.

TO FRANCE.

Some of us used to say in later days that for purely futile discomfort none of our experiences in France beat the Divisional training at Tidworth; and whether this was so or not, there is no doubt that most of us were thoroughly glad to see the end of the training and the suspense and the farewells, and to feel the train moving out of Tidworth Station in the early morning of November 16th, 1915. Snow fell as we marched out of barracks, led by a Cavalry band, and shouted Good-bye-ee to the fluttering handkerchiefs in upper windows along the street; but everybody was cheerful—except Major Rostron's servant, staggering on to the platform under the largest green canvas kit-bag ever seen—and Mrs. Barker, Mrs. Powlett, and Mrs. Banbury were there to distribute newspapers, and General Kellett, too, waving his hand as the train moved off and the band played " Auld Lang Syne."

The Battalion went in two halves, and the transport, under Captain Gell, had started a day earlier by Southampton and Havre. After a long halt at Ashford—a station of no repute in railway circles—we at last reached Folkestone after sunset, and embarked; an excellent crossing, with only the mildest swell on the water, and just enough moonlight to see the grey forms of T.B.D.'s slinking along beside us; smoking and talking were forbidden; and though we were blissfully unconscious of danger, a hospital ship on the same course struck a mine only a few hours later.

Boulogne at its worst—muddy cobbles, deep puddles, a crowd of men who had been waiting four days for a leave-boat, endless embarkation officers ! And the rest camp to which we marched— K Camp, Ostrohove Camp ! The curses of the innumerable battalions which had rested there had fallen upon it; and no one to greet us at midnight but a drunken man at the Q.M. Stores, who was prepared to issue as many damp and lousy blankets as were required ! It was a vile welcome to France; but the next morning when the sun was shining on the rain-swept, wind-swept scene, things looked more cheerful. Platoons were having rifle inspection, cooks were lighting fires, permanently 'fatigue' men from other units were roadmaking, officers' servants were busy on an irrigation scheme among the eight sodden and tattered tents (a scheme, that is to say, for diverting the water from one tent into the next), and some of us were trying our French on certain old women and children who carried chocolate and little cakes in basket-trays.

27

In a letter announcing our safe arrival at Boulogne, the C.O. wrote to the Mayor of Kensington, "We are all immensely happy, and the men love hearing the sound of the guns at night. One man wrote in a letter I had to censor, 'I am writing this on the back of a dead German.'"

We were glad to leave Ostrohove Camp on the 18th, and to march to the station at Pont aux Briques, where a huge train rolled in to receive us, and revealed to our delighted eyes our transport safely re-united to us. At St. Omer at 6 p.m. we got orders to detrain at Steenbecque, a little further on; and thence the battalion, unquenchably cheerful, marched through the night and the execrable puddles, dropping a platoon here and a platoon there as the interpreters directed, till it had dwindled to D Company and H.Q.; and the latter having invaded the Maire's farmhouse, D Company vanished alone into the darkness.

The strength of the Battalion was 30 officers and 992 other ranks. Lieut.-Colonel R. Barnett Barker was in command, Major H. Rostron (from the 5th D.G.'s) was second in command, and Capt. W. J. Phythian-Adams Adjutant. Capt. G. W. Daman commanded A Company, Major B. W. Williams-Powlett B Company, Capt. A. MacDougall C Company, and Major T. H. Boardman D Company. With the 17th R.Fus., the 23rd R.Fus., and 24th R.Fus., we formed the 99th Infantry Brigade, under Brigadier-General R. O. Kellett, in the 33rd Division; but at noon on November 25th the Brigade was transferred, in a happy moment, to the 2nd Division in the First Army. This was during the march southwards to Bethune, by way of Thiennes, Cantraine, and St. Venant (where we first saw English beer in the shop windows). At Bethune, then almost untouched except in the main square, the Battalion was billeted in the Ecole des Jeunes Filles. Have they now returned, those jeunes filles, to that noble building, those chaste class-rooms, that spacious play-ground, those altogether wonderful underground baths? Or was the whole place shattered, like the rest of Bethune, in the spring of 1918? Anyhow, our first visit was for one night only, and the next morning we were off, in rain that had turned to snow before we were out of the town, along the road to Beuvry and Annequin, trudging under heavy packs through the slush on the unsympathetic pavé, spattered with mud from passing lorries, and realizing, as we proceeded from Beuvry by platoons at 100 yards interval and met one of the 98th Brigade battalions coming away, morose and fagged out, from the trenches, that we were really in the war zone. During the next twelve days our education in trench warfare was begun. Billeted in the ruined

28

houses of Annequin South, we sent up companies or platoons or working parties every day to the trenches, to learn what shell fire and rifle fire were like, and communication trenches knee-deep in mud and collapsed traverses and crumbling parapets. Many of the men had not had dry feet since leaving England. On November 29th, Lieut. W. A. Murray started his score of wound stripes with a scratch on the wrist; two days later a shell descended from a high angle on to C Company's cooker, which was behind a wall, and blew it to pieces without much damage to Pte. Glinwood, who was sitting on it; and on December 5th a whizz-bang fell on a section of B Company in the road, killing Pte. Edgington and wounding ten men. On the 9th the Battalion marched back through the outskirts of Bethune to the friendly little village of Fouquereuil, to rest and to have its first lesson in gas-drill, by passing through a tent filled with chlorine, in the partly submerged sports field of Bethune. The 2nd Division was at this time re-arranged, so as to leaven the raw units with the veterans of Mons; and in exchange for the 17th and 24th R.Fus. which went to the 5th Inf. Bde., the 99th Inf. Bde. received the 1st K.R.R.C. and 1st R. Berks.

From Fouquereuil the Battalion went back to Annequin on the 15th, and into the trenches for the first time on the 17th, in fine weather, and out again three days later. Christmas Day was spent in the front line, but on Boxing Day we went back to Annequin for Christmas dinners, and on the 29th marched 10 miles to L'Eclème, a straggling village in a network of irrigation channels. Perhaps the signallers have not forgotten their billet at Annequin, in the loft of the washerwoman's house; nor the Christmas dinner downstairs, with festoons of paper flowers and lanterns, and a mountain of beer bottles, fruit and cigars on the side table. And C Company may remember the mine scare in the front line on Christmas Eve, and the tap-tapping which the tunnelling experts declared to be the dripping of water and not the picks of the Hun. Poor Harris was blinded by a sniper when on sentry-go, and Vango was shot dead on Christmas Day in the morning. But on the whole our casualties were not heavy during our first tours of the trenches.

After a dull fortnight of bad weather at L'Eclème, the Battalion marched back by Essars towards the trenches—on the north of the canal this time—and took over the line at Festubert on January 18th, 1916. Instead of trenches there were solid high breast-works, with plenty of duck-boards for the support, while the front was held by a series of islands or "grouse-butts," in which the men were relieved every twenty-four hours, no communication being possible in day light. Captain H. S. Goodwin was wounded on the 21st while walking up the Quinque Rue; and there were a few casualties in the grouse-butts; but for the most part life was lazy and innocuous; warm sunny days and misty nights. A shell fell on the roof of the bomb-store and shifted eight boxes and smashed the beams without exploding anything. Leave had begun for officers and men—a great stimulant to cheerfulness. The C.O., immaculately dressed in his best clothes, had to accompany the Brigadier round the line just before he started on leave. General Kellett wanted to see everything; clambered out over the breast-work to see the field of fire of our machine guns, and led his escort no end of a dance, till at last the Boche could not resist the temptation to snipe at the party with whizz-bangs. Alas! the first one surprised our C.O. in the act of crossing a plank over a stream, and he lost his footing—and had to go on leave in his second-best clothes, much to the amusement of the Brigadier.

After a week in Divisional Reserve at Hingettes, the Battalion went into the line again at Givenchy on February 3rd, historic trenches and redoubts and mine-craters, with a picturesque "village line" of battered houses—including the most famous Windy Corner. The 6th Royal Irish Rifles, under the gallant Major Redmond, were attached to us for trench instruction, and caused a certain amount of amusement and anxiety; their officers *would* sleep with their boots off, and their sentries were seldom on the fire-step. But their R.S.M., accompanying Colonel Barker on his nightly rounds, used to plead for them. "Don't be hard on the bhoys, sir—don't, now!" It was at Givenchy, too, that, after a succession of failures, we got a really splendid M.O. in Captain W. A. Miller, who had been with the 1st K.R.R.C. earlier in the war, and was as fine a fighter as a doctor; and a really splendid Transport Officer in Lieut. J. Ross, from the 16th Lancers.

The following extract from a letter written by Paul Destrubé, huddled up in the corner of a Givenchy dug-out, will recall the memory of that gallant trio of brothers who made so much history for the Battalion, and will give a brilliant picture of trench-life for those readers who never experienced it. "This sand-bag abode is feebly illuminated by a candle dimly burning. My neighbour, who is yet more uncomfortably cramped up, is falling off to sleep, and his muddy, unshaven and jam-smeared face is resting on my shoulder. Occasionally he grunts vigorously, making the paper I am writing upon flutter. I've just removed an open tin of jam from under the mud-clotted boot of the fellow opposite me. A fair-sized piece of cheese is pinned to the sand-bagged wall by means of a cartridge.

The bread has all been devoured, but a few broken pieces of hard tack biscuits lie scattered somewhere on the ground beneath this living, semi-sleeping entanglement of men. A bayonet thrust in the wall serves as a candlestick, and the candlegrease is slowly but persistently dripping on the fellow's forehead who is sleeping directly beneath. With one finger I could swing the bayonet slightly to one side—but I am not going to do so, because it would be a pity to destroy such a charming situation. I'm almost hypnotised as I watch the grease slowly dripping—drip, drip, drip—and still he sleeps !......
And so we are here, huddled and interlaced together, strangers all, until we met in this common cause: in this circle of six we once represented such a different type, but now all gradually approaching the same—the man in his primitive stage.........But my reflections have been disturbed; my neighbour is responsible for more grunts, and furthermore he's tried to stretch himself. There !—I thought so—he's kicked the fellow opposite in the stomach, and now they are both grunting. All is quiet again, the dirty, unkissable face is in its old position again—on my shoulder."

On the 16th we trekked back by Le Quesnoy and Gonnehem to Ham-en-Artois, where deep snow prevented exercise, and the fighting at Verdun kept us on short notice to move. Our orders came on the 27th, and on the next day the Battalion marched to Barlin, a mining village, where we were not over-welcome at first. French troops holding this part of the line were being withdrawn, and on March 3rd we relieved the 135th Regiment of the French Army in the hutments in Bois de Noulette. They trailed off into the night, carrying lanterns, and left us to clean up; but when the sun shone many happy days were spent in that wood and in the village of Bouvigny behind—and, for that matter, in the front line, too, close to ruined Souchez—which Kensington has now " adopted "—and opposite the Bois en Hache. This was the battlefield of May, 1915, when the French drove the Germans off the Lorette Ridge and nearly took Lens; ten months later the ground was still strewn with *débris* and corpses, and one of our Company headquarters, in a railway cutting, had been the German General's Headquarters, as proved by the wall-papers and furniture in the dug-out. We were confronted by a difficult situation, because the front line was totally cut off from the support line in daylight, and was enfiladed from the German trenches on the Vimy Ridge on our right. The German front line opposite us was only thirty or forty yards away; No Man's Land was a mass of wire entanglements, and a mutual understanding between the French and the Germans had reduced offensive warfare to a farce. We were obliged to conform to this arrangement till we could improve the trenches and repair the C.T.'s; and there was little or no firing, even at night. By day German officers and men might be seen sitting on the parapet, laughing, shouting, gesticulating; and a certain degree of fraternisation between sentries in saps only a few yards apart was inevitable. The Brigade Intelligence sent English newspapers to be thrown across into the German trenches for propaganda purposes. But gradually the activity increased, chiefly owing to our 2nd Division artillery, which was calculated to turn the most peaceful part of the line into a hornet's nest; and by the time that we left the sector in the middle of May, life was by no means as easy as at first.

For the most part we had wonderful spring weather, and plenty of time in which to enjoy it; but the actual trenches were in a very bad state and the open country over which all movement was done was full of bogs. On April 26th there was a slight patrol affray near the railway station, and Lt. E. C. Rossell gained the first Military Cross for the battalion : and at Bouvigay Major Rostron's terrier Romp, slayer of a thousand rats, was stolen—presumably by gunners. But the happiest days were spent at Ourton, near Bruay, a little village with a stream and charming billets and charming inhabitants, where the Battalion rested behind the line for two spells, and young men's fancies were diverted by the spring weather from thoughts of war. It was at the end of the second spell, after some Brigade manœuvres at Bomy, and an inspection by Sir Henry Wilson, then commanding the Fourth Corps, that the Battalion, having gone to Hersin, a mining village, was suddenly whisked away in motor-buses to retrieve the positions on the Vimy Ridge from which the Germans had just driven the 47th Division. From Souchez in the valley we had often watched mines being exploded on the ridge on our right—an amazingly fine spectacle from a safe distance; and now on May 22nd it was our job to relieve the 17th London Regiment in the Talus des Zouaves and to attack almost at once, at 1.30 a.m. on the 23rd. These orders were cancelled, and the attack postponed to 8.25 p.m., in conjunction with the 1st R. Berks. on our right and the 20th London Regiment on our left. Col. Barker was temporarily in command of the Brigade at Cabaret Rouge, Major Rostron of the Battalion. The enemy got news of our intentions and put down a heavy barrage, which prevented the Berks. from forming up for the attack, and at 8.15 p.m., Major Rostron being informed that he would be unsupported on his right, cancelled the advance. The message to this effect did not reached B. Company, under Captain Banbury, which went forward, took the German trench, set to work to consolidate it, and stayed there, under command of Lt. R. H. Gregg, for an hour and a half, till recalled by Capt. Miller, the M.O., who was out looking for wounded and who found the lost Company. The casualties in this very gallant and unfortunate adventure were heavy : Capt. Banbury wounded, and Lt. C. J. Fowler, who died in hospital on June 1st : 7 other ranks killed, including Sgt. Drew and Pte. van Tromp, and 78 wounded. The hardest work of all was carrying the wounded back to Cabaret Rouge the next morning, when the Battalion was relieved : but at any rate we all felt that, as General Kellett said, B. Company had saved the honour of the Brigade. For this action Capt. Miller got the D.S.O., Lt. Gregg the M.C., and Sgt. Fisher, Sgt. Wheeler, L.-Cpl. W. H. Metcalfe and Pte. Webb the D.C.M.

For the next seven weeks the Battalion remained in the Vimy sector, with occasional rests at Villers-au-Bois or Camblain L'Abbé or Maisnil Bouché. Many new officers and drafts joined : Major C. C. Harman succeeded Major Rostron as second in command; but on the other hand there were casualties. Capt. J. H. E. Woods and Capt. Hicks were wounded and never rejoined; while on June 21st Capt. G. D. A. Black was killed by a rifle grenade. In him and in Lt. Fowler the Battalion lost two young and brilliant officers who could never be replaced in the more strenuous days to come.

With July came the beginning of the Somme Battle, and it was only a question of time before the 2nd Division would be needed to take its share in the fighting; but day followed anxious day, and it was not till the 20th that the Battalion entrained at Diéval and went south to Amiens, and marched—oh, that grilling, unforgetable march !—through Corbie to Morlancourt, and thence to bivouac at the Sandpits on the 23rd, en route for Montauban and Delville Wood. At last the time had come, after eight months of gradual preparation and initiation, during which the Roll of Honour counted just over fifty names ! At the Divine Service held by Padre St. John in the open air at the Sandpits, we felt more keenly than ever before, that we were on the edge of the whirlpool : and that within a week that Roll of Honour might be doubled in length and in glory. But it was typical of the spirit of the Battalion that when the Brigadier, haranguing us on the 22nd, said that the officers were like shepherds, and that if one was killed, the sheep must choose another shepherd and follow him, C Company lost no time in labelling their sergeants' mess " The Shepherds' Rest," and the little bivouacs as " Sheep-pens."

CHAPTER III.

DELVILLE WOOD AND THE ANCRE.

"Let whoso will forget it,
   Walking life's noisy ways :
   We who have looked on the Reapers
   Go quietly all our days."

It is a pity, from the picturesque point of view, that in some of the fights in which the Battalion took part it had the bad luck to be given the less distinguished task of supporting or reinforcing the actual assaulting troops. When the Brigade attacked Delville Wood, in the Ancre fighting of November, at Miraumont in February, 1917, and in the Moeuvres battle of November 30th, to the superficial observer it might appear that the 22nd R. Fusiliers was allotted a task less exacting than that of the other battalions in the Brigade. But our comrades of the 23rd R. Fusiliers, the 1st R. Berks. and the 1st K.R.R.C., would be the first to acknowledge that in every big fight all the troops involved, whether in the limelight or just out of it, were equally tested; that in every advance the 22nd R. Fusiliers was engaged up to the hilt before the end of the fight, and that in no case did we ever fail to do the utmost in our power for the honour of the Brigade. Delville Wood is a notable illustration of this unobstrusive efficiency. When the attack began two of our companies were under the Staff Captain as carrying parties, the other two were Brigade Reserve : but by the end of the day every available man had been thrown into the fight, and but for our help the right flank of the wood might never have been held. Our casualties tell their own tale. Between July 24th and August 6th we lost one officer and 56 other ranks killed, 7 officers and 203 other ranks wounded.

From Sandpit Valley the Battalion started at 8 p.m. on July 24th to march to Montauban, the village which had been captured by the 11th Battalion on July 1st within 25 minutes of zero, and by 3 a.m. on the 25th the companies had been accommodated in Montauban Alley and the forward edge of the village. The march had been exhausting and exciting, through the old front lines and into the tortured, littered area of the stinking

34

battle ground : such artillery fire, such débris, such smells, such confusion were all new experiences, and to these were added during the next few days the whirr and plop of tear-shells and gas-shells to add to the general discomfort. Major Harman was made Commandant of Montauban, and the officers of the Battalion were as follows :—H.Q., Col. Barker commanding; Capt. Phythian Adams adjutant; M.O., Capt. Miller; Chaplain, Padre St. John; Lewis Gun Officer, Lt. Parks; Signalling Officer, Lt. Stone; A Company, Capt. Clifford, Lts. Roscoe, Murray, Simons and Powles; B Company, Capt. Walsh, Lts. Gibson, Worship and Martin; C Company, Capt. MacDougall, Lts. Ling, Walker and Gould; D Company, Capt. Gell, Lts. Powell, Durand, Hutcheson and Pimm. The weather was hot and dry, with morning mists; and from Montauban it was possible to look across the valley to High Wood away on the left, to Longueval and Delville Wood in front and to Waterlot Farm and Guillemont on the right. In the valley, which was constantly shelled by the enemy, our field guns flashed and barked day and night, but most of our batteries were behind Montauban.

At 3 a.m. on the 27th C and D Companies moved to some trenches in the valley, and H.Q. to a ditch at the road-side near the bottom of Bernafay Wood : while A and B Companies were organised into carrying parties by the Staff Captain, Capt. Allfrey. After an hour's bombardment by 369 guns on the Wood, the barrage lifted at 7.10 a.m. for the 23rd R. Fusiliers and 1st K.R.R.C. to advance, supported by the 1st R. Berks., and by 10 a.m. the German prisoners were beginning to reach the Dressing Station and our H.Q. at Bernafay in great numbers—some with shocking bayonet wounds, but most of them merely scared and thoroughly glad to be nearly out of danger. As the day wore on the difficulties in Delville Wood increased; Capt. Walsh collected all the carrying parties and went to help the 23rd R. Fusiliers, and Capt. Gell took C and D Companies up to the Wood, and held the S.W. flank of it, which was seriously threatened by counter-attacks. Capt. C. B. Grant, a 22nd R. Fusilier man, who was in command of the Brigade Machine Gun Company, covered himself with glory on that day, and was killed while placing his guns—a charming and intrepid young officer—said to be the only man who had ever alarmed General Kellett by his daring. Four officers were wounded that day; 26 other ranks were killed, including Sgt. Wiles, Sgt. Keen, Sgt. Lawton and Cpl. Haddock, and such well-known figures as Penwarden and Markie; 143 wounded, 20 unaccounted for. The only communication trench to the Wood, Longueval Alley, was a shambles, full of dead or sleeping men, and the open ground was swept by shell-fire continuously; so that the exhaustion of carrying parties can be neither imagined nor described. On the 29th the Battalion, now consisting of 18 officers and 400 other ranks, was withdrawn to Bund Trench, the old German front line near Mametz, bare and dusty and full of shell-holes and barbed wire, where some of the men splashed about in the water at the bottom of a mine-crater, and Sunday, the 30th, became a real day of rest for body and mind.

On the night of August 1st/2nd the Battalion took over Delville Wood from the 1st Kings; the 23rd R. Fusiliers were in support and Col. Barker was in command of the whole wood. The march up there was long and trying, and a section under Lt. H. A. Holmes was blown up by a shell; the 1st Kings were almost demoralised by the terrible ordeal of the last few days, and the relief was not over till daylight. A and D Companies held the front line, such as it was, facing north, with B Company in close support; C. Company held the right flank of the wood facing east, with Lewis Gun posts to fill the gaps. The Devil's Wood had fairly earned its name : from the air it was reported to be totally destroyed; on the ground it was one vast tangle of fallen trees, full of fragments of crumbled trenches and " scrapes," full of German dead and South Africans and our own men, upon whose tortured bodies the summer heat had wrought its alchemy. The wood was exposed to shell fire from three directions, and the enemy was known to be holding the fringe of it in front; from all sorts of unexpected corners and scraps of cover the rattle of a machine gun or the crack of the sniper's rifle kept our men ever on the alert, as it was ideal ground for " infiltration," and no one knew when a company might find itself totally surrounded by creeping Boches. In the late afternoon of the 3rd a message came from neighbouring troops in Longueval that large numbers of Germans had been seen entering the Wood opposite our front; this news was forwarded to our front companies by telephone, and sure enough presently a heavy barrage came down on the near edge of the Wood and on Battalion H.Q. The front line telephoned that Germans were advancing through the undergrowth, and at that moment the telephone line was cut. Great excitement; machine gun fire in the Wood, gun fire, pandemonium. The S.O.S. rocket was fired from Battalion H.Q. trench to rouse our gunners, and all H.Q. lined the parapet in the dusk, expecting to see the Germans come tumbling out of the Wood. But nothing happened: the noise gradually quietened down. The Battalion had "repelled a serious counter-attack." But only those who were in the front line can tell whether they were really attacked at all; certainly no German ever reached their trench, and some people even go so far as to say that the troops seen in the dusk advancing shoulder to shoulder through the undergrowth were the fabulous creations of over-wrought nerves. But at any rate this incident illustrates the eeriness and devilry of the Wood; and the casualties prove it the death-trap that it was.

On the night of August 3rd the Battalion was relieved by the 1st R. Berks., and on the following night the Wood was handed over by them to the 17th Division; so that it remains true for all time that the 99th Brigade took and held Delville Wood and never lost it again. The relief of the 3rd had its peculiar tragedies for us, in that Capt. Alan MacDougall and C.S.M. Evans, the two mainstays of C Company, two of the finest fellows that ever lived, were killed in the Wood after the relief was complete. The remnants of the Battalion trailed back to Bund Trench, and on the 5th were moved further back behind the guns into the area of the sausage balloons near the Citadel. The M.O. as usual had performed prodigies during the fight; and he stayed behind afterwards to take carrying parties up into the Wood to search for wounded, in some ways perhaps the most exacting duty of all under heavy shell-fire. He it was who recognised Capt. MacDougall's boot sticking out of the ground, dug the body out and brought it back to be buried in the little cemetery at the Citadel on the 6th, in the presence of the General and a large company of mourners. It is perhaps as well to note that Capt. Miller was recommended again for the V.C.: this was the second time, but he never got it, and ended the war with a D.S.O. and M.C., which only faintly reflect his bravery. Naturally the decorations awarded for Delville Wood were quite inadequate— *everyone* deserved a medal—and Col. Barker did his utmost to see that justice was done to his beloved Battalion.

It was peaceful at the Citadel, except one morning when a H.V. shell blew the Staff Captain's tent sky-high while it was empty and wounded slightly one of our officers about 400 yards away; and a few minutes later the Battalion was regaled by the sight of the Brigadier, in pyjamas and the highest spirits, being whirled past in a motor car to a safer retreat for his breakfast. We had time to clean up and write home and consider the future; and it is typical of the havoc wrought by Delville Wood that out of 30 trained signallers brought from England eight months ago,

37

only 6 now remained to form the nucleus of a new section. In looking back at the panorama of those months there is an unwarlike figure which comes very pleasantly into the memory—always welcome and always turning up, whether on Vimy Ridge or in Delville Wood, with the ration parties or ahead of them—the postman, Corporal Howe. He never failed us, and his memory deserves a special word of thanks.

One morning the King motored past our bivouacs: the Divisional General, Major-General W. G. Walker, V.C., C.B., inspected and thanked the Brigade; there were strong rumours that we were going back to the sea-side for a long rest and that leave would reopen; drafts from the reserve battalion at Edinburgh began to arrive; there were aquatic sports and water polo when the Battalion was bivouacking by a river, and on Sunday, August 13th (always a Sunday!) a train journey to Amiens and a ten mile march to Vaux for four days; then off by route march north-east-wards to join the 5th Corps (General Fanshawe) of the 5th Army (General Gough), and on the 18th the Battalion relieved the 2nd Scots Guards in the front line at Hebuterne. Here were well-revetted trenches, a peaceful routine enlivened by trench mortar strafes, the carrying of innumerable gas cylinders to the front line, the digging of Fusilier trench, and the remarkably successful raid of a small party under 2/Lt. Martin on September 15th, when ten prisoners were taken without any casualties on our side. There was a bombing accident at Couin, in which Lt. Ling was wounded; and the neighbouring village of Coigneux was practically destroyed by the explosion of an ammunition dump, in which our Brigadier's son was killed. Another casualty which should be recorded was P. W. Fisher, a very fine sergeant, who had been given a commission only a month earlier and was killed on patrol by a machine gun bullet. There were regimental sports on the 25th at Authie, when the Battalion came out of the line. Major Harman went away to command a Battalion of the Hants Regiment and Capt. Phythian Adams was promoted to be second in command.

Meanwhile the sound of heavy bombardments to the south day and night was a warning that there was still plenty of fighting to be done; and as the English advance south of the Ancre River progressed, so the German salient north of the river—with its nose at Beaumont Hamel—became more pronounced. The 5th Army was deputed to deal with this salient, which had proved impreg-nable at the first attack on July 1st and had been steadily strengthened ever since by the enemy. But the weather was

38

against us. A very wet autumn had set in, and no one who was with the Battalion in those days is likely to forget the state of the trenches in the Serre-Redan sector, and the almost unbearable dreariness and discomfort of those Acheux Wood days. The " tours " were reduced to two days, but this did not help much, as the exhaustion of reliefs was increased. The numbers of the Battalion dwindled in spite of every effort to maintain health. After one tour of the trenches, two hundred men turned up at sick parade in Mailly Maillet the next morning. When the Battalion rested at Acheux Wood no exercise was possible; the huts stood in a sea of mud, connected with duck-board tracks, and the Colonel used to take a daily tramp up and down the twenty yards of deserted railway platform of the village station. To add to all these trials, there was the suspense of the imminent fighting. Zero day was postponed over and over again; the plans for the attack altered and enlarged; the attack itself practised, whenever dry ground could be obtained, over dummy trenches. New ideas of " battle order," bomb-carriers, distinctive badges, etc., were dished out to the men till everyone was heartily sick of the battle long before it began. There was, at any rate, no excuse of not being prepared for it, or of not knowing the various objectives—the violet, green, yellow, blue and brown lines, which may be studied with the story of the battle in the *History of the Second Division*. This is only an account of the share which the 22nd R. Fusiliers took in the events of November 13-16.

The Battalion assembled in battle order at Bertrancourt on the 12th, and at 1.30 a.m. on the 13th started in the darkness to march into the trenches via Mailly Maillet. The following officers were present :—H.Q., Lt.-Col. Barnett Barker, Major Phythian-Adams, Lt. Stone, Capt. Miller, R.A.M.C., and Lt. E. J. Pimm (Lewis Gun Officer); A Company, Capt. Roscoe, Lts. Simons, Thornhill and Hallett; B Company, Capt. Gregg, Lts. G. H. Evans, Perraton and Fitton; C Company, Capt. Gell, Lts. Kelly, F. Adams and Pignon; D Company, Major Walsh, Capt. Powell, Lts. Parks and Hutcheson. The whole Battalion formed up in the long communicating trench Sixth Avenue in the order A B C D Companies, and waited for the 5th Infantry Brigade to move out of the forward trenches to the attack. Zero hour was at 5.45 a.m., at which instant every gun from the Ancre to far north of us opened the bombardment. It was terrific : and so was the enemy's retort. Immediately the Battalion moved forward turning right and left into the old British front and support lines as they

39

became empty, while H.Q. went to the White City—a very different scene from the courts and palaces of 1914 memories.

At 4.30 p.m. C and B Companies, under Major Phythian-Adams, were sent across No Man's Land to form a defensive flank facing northwards to cover the exposed flank of the 5th Infantry Brigade, who were holding the first objective. They were joined at 4 a.m. on the 14th by A and D Companies. The confusion in the network of old German trenches was considerable, but a flank was made by 9 a.m. and held under heavy shell-fire all through the 14th. There remained however a gallant party of Germans in the Quadrilateral, a cluster of trenches on high ground to the north, and orders were received to evict them on the morning of the 15th with the aid of two tanks. These novelties however stuck in the mud in No Man's Land; so bombing parties of A, B and D Companies advanced without them. By noon considerable progress had been made, the position, mostly of machine gun and Lewis gun posts, being over the crest of the high ground and dominating the whole Quadrilateral. It was held and consolidated : the whole of a post of C Company was obliterated by shell-fire at one time, but the survivors never lost their steadiness for an instant under the most trying conditions of mud, cold, exposure, shell-fire and shortage of water and rations. Towards dawn on the 16th relief by the 15th H.L.I. began and was completed by 7.30 a.m., when the remnants of the Companies went back through the sunshine of a beautiful autumn morning to billets in Mailly Maillet.

So ended the battle of the Ancre, not less exacting than that of Delville, though fought under very different conditions. The Battalion had every reason to be proud of its achievements and to accept the thanks of the Commander-in-Chief at Gezaincourt a few days later. It had endured much and fought well at the end of a most trying ordeal; and considering all things the casualties were light. One officer, 2/Lt. Fitton was killed, Capt Gell, Capt. Miller, Lts. Parks and Hutcheson wounded : of other ranks 19 were killed, 56 wounded and 7 missing. Among the dead was Sgt. H. Munro (" Saki ") a very gallant gentleman, who brought as much honour to the Battalion as that other self-effacing scholar, L. G. Russel-Davies, who had been killed in the blowing in of a dug-out a month before.

The following letter from the G.O.C. 6th Infantry Brigade, to whom the Battalion was attached during the fight, shows more clearly the value of the work done. It is dated 16/11/16.

"My dear Barker,

"I must just write you a few lines to express, as well as I can, my thanks and admiration of the really splendid work of your Battalion during the last three days. I really don't know how we should have got on if I had not had the good fortune to be lent the 22nd Royal Fusiliers. As you know, at the time you joined us, the 6th Brigade mustered, for fighting purposes, at the most some 600 rifles, and we should have been sorely put to it to deal with the Quadrilateral situation, in fact I doubt if we could have done anything of an offensive nature. My most grateful thanks (in the name of the whole Brigade) to you and Major Adams and, if your Brigadier has no objection, would you take steps to convey my statements of esteem and admiration to all ranks of the Battalion ? I hope your casualties were not very heavy. I hope to see you soon and thank you in person. Yours very sincerely, A. C. Dale."

The Battalion marched back by easy stages to Yvrench, a village near Abbeville, where, with good billets, estaminets, Sgt. McGowan's baths and a liberal leave-allotment, a very memorable Christmas was spent. Cigarettes and pipes from the Mayor of Kensington, plum puddings and £5 a Company from Mrs. Barker, added to other gifts, spurred everyone to great efforts; the billets were decorated like fairy grottoes, and the Divisional police were wisely invited to join the banquet; so no one got into any trouble.

CHAPTER IV.

MIRAUMONT AND OPPY.

The year 1917 started with the Battalion in splendid condition, made up to full strength with some very fine drafts, and well rested after the rigours of 1916. Great kudos was won by a platoon demonstration at Yvrench under command of Lt. G. H. Evans, and the whole of the 5th Army was instructed to model itself upon the same lines. But the time came to move on to fresh adventures, and on January 9th the Battalion started to march to Candas, Beauquesne and Senlis, reached on the 13th. The weather was bad, and after a week of separation in which the companies were working under the R.E.'s round Aveluy—just north of Albert—they reassembled at Bouzincourt, and on the 28th, a week later, relieved the 1st Kings in Wolfe Huts on the Albert-Bapaume road, in support, with A Company at the Red Chateau at Courcelette. This was all country captured from the enemy since July 1st, desolate, treeless, a mass of mine craters, shell holes and wire entanglements, with a few repaired roads and beaten tracks to link up the hut camps with the front area. The trenches in front of Courcelette were isolated fragments of old battered trenches reclaimed and made into posts—often without even a dug-out; there were no communication trenches; and the intense cold of that February is a thing to be remembered with horror. The C.O. had rightly prided himself on the success of his efforts to prevent "trench feet": thousands of pairs of socks to supplement the Army issue had been sent from Kensington, and every man elaborately trained in foot massage; so that it is safe to say that the cases of "trench foot" in 1916 had been negligible. But at Courcelette the struggle became almost too hard, and some cases were admitted, in spite of the M.O.'s disgust, to hospital. One man died of the cold at Bouzincourt. The second in command spent nearly all his time at Wolfe Huts in superintending the gradual thawing of Perrier bottles round a Canadian stove. Even eggs froze hard! The misery of days of forced inaction in the front line may be imagined: and with the ground hard as iron and often coated with ice, the walk to the trenches was very trying, especially as very few shells were "duds."

We were now south of the Ancre and Beaumont Hamel. Preparations were made to attack the Germans in the direction of Miraumont. In General Kellett's absence Colonel Barker had to command the Brigade; Major-General Pereira had succeeded Major-General Walker in command of the 2nd Division in December, and we were in the 2nd Corps (Lieut.-General C. W. Jacob.) A few days before the great fight the Battalion lost its best officer in Capt. R. L. Roscoe, M.C., "under 20, with a brain of 40, and a born soldier," as the C.O. wrote. He was hit by a shell while asleep in his "serape" at A. Company H.Q.'s one afternoon. A message came by "power-buzzer-"— a new invention—to Battalion H.Q. and Capt. Coad, who had succeeded Capt. Miller as M.O., set off with stretcher bearers over the open in daylight, and brought him back safely: but he died in hospital. He was the last of the officers who had been with the Battalion since the White City days, excepting the Colonel and Major Phythian-Adams. Lt.-Col. G. G. A. Hankey, commanding the 3rd Battalion Royal Sussex, was a visitor during these days and saw a good deal of active warfare, as the 1st Royal Berks executed a brilliant raid from our lines on the night of February 5/6th, bringing back 50 prisoners. This was a prelude to the big attack of the 17th. On the previous afternoon B Company was attached to 1st K.R.R.C., and at 9.30 p.m. the other three companies proceeded to battle positions between the East and West Miraumont roads. D Company was to form a defensive flank on the right across No Man's Land as the 23rd Royal Fusiliers advanced: A and C were to attack the third objective, the Brown Line, while B was helping the 1st K.R.R.C. on the left and also carrying ammunition for the machine gun company. The following officers went into action:—H.Q. in West Miraumont dug-out, Major Phythian-Adams, Major Gregg, Capt. Stone, Capt. Coad, R.A.M.C., Capt. St. John. C.F.; A Company, Capt. N. S. Powell, Lts. Payne, Goodman and Lawrence; B Company, Lts. Perraton, E. A. Burgess; C Company, Capt. Simons, Lts. Pignon, Ellison and Boulton; D Company, Major Walsh, Lts. Saword, G. H. Evans and Fuller. Liaison officers with flank units, Lts. T. H. Evans and Thornhill. Lewis gun officer, Lt. Pimm.

The thaw had come suddenly and the mud was appalling. It was still dark when the attack began at 5.45 a.m. on the 17th, and as the enemy had been warned by deserters (from another unit of course!) his barrage came down at 5 a.m., especially round the shell holes occupied by D Company, and his machine guns began to rattle at 5.30 a.m. D Company went through this, but found the enemy wire uncut and protected by an unexpected machine gun. Major Walsh was mortally wounded and Capt. Evans also put out of action. Sgt. Palmer, with six other men, cut his way through the wire and rushed the trench, making a block in it. Sgt. Brown, who had been hit in the stomach, was taken down a dug-out to die. Above, in the trench, desperate fighting went on all the morning. Palmer and his gang repulsed seven separate counter-attacks of bombs, rifle and machine gun fire. At last his bombs were exhausted and he went off to fetch more from H.Q. : and while he was away the post was driven in. On his return he organised his party again, and though badly shaken by a bomb explosion, drove back the Germans and restored the very important flank guard. For his good work on this day he was awarded the V.C., and the rest of his party got D.C.M.'s or M.M.'s.

It is curious, in view of the popular estimate of German chivalry, to record that during the short time that the post was in the enemy's hands, Sgt. Brown was removed from the dug-out and carried back to German hospitals to be healed of his wound. Honour to whom honour is due ! But, indeed, of this fight, the Colonel wrote :—" Unfortunately we bumped into real Huns, who fought splendidly and cleanly—not like the miserable creatures we whistled out of dug-outs at the Ancre battle. They came at us like tigers and never let us alone." The mist that hung over the battlefield all day had only one advantage—it enabled the stretcher parties to clear the forward area of wounded; but in other ways it was disastrous. It hampered the artillery and prevented any observation; and when the time came for A and C Companies to advance on the third objective, they lost direction and went too much to the left across the front of the famous Boom Ravine. Capt. Powell discovered his mistake in time, and extricated A Company; but Capt. Simons with one platoon of C Company went " into the blue," and was no more heard of. Very few of them were taken prisoner unwounded, and the deeds that were done that day when the Germans swarmed out of the mist in an outflanking counter-attack, were worthy of the Battalion. By noon there were only three unwounded officers in the front line, Lts. Saword, Pimm and Perraton : and the toll of the men, especially of the Lewis gunners, was on the same scale, something like 75 per cent. There were 85 men killed—such unforgettable heroes as Sgt. Hennessey, Sgt. Brierley and the two remaining Destrubés among them. But the survivors of the Lewis

44

gun detachments were worthy of them, and came staggering out of the fight with 8 of their 14 guns. There was a funeral service for Major Walsh at Ovillers cemetery on the 21st, Ash Wednesday, and subsequently a large cross was made by the pioneers and inscribed to the memory of all our officers and men who fell in that battle. We were in huts just across the road, busy refitting and training new specialists, when the news of the enemy's retreat reached us. The attack of the 17th, failure as it was, had taught him a lesson; and the difficult work of following him, and giving him another prod, occupied the Division. The prod which drove him out of Grevillers Trench and Loupart Wood on March 10th was given by the Brigade, but the rôle of the 22nd was only to carry stores forward. For several nights previously there were carrying parties to make dumps for the attack, and Lt. D. H. Wright was in charge of the Brigade bomb store. The attack was very successful, the "Lady's Leg" being rushed with typical gallantry by the 23rd Royal Fusiliers. Within an hour of zero our carrying parties had stocked the enemy trench with bombs and S.A.A.: but there was always more to be carried, and at dusk, when the 22nd was ordered to go forward to dig a new trench, the men were fairly exhausted. No. 1 Company—the Battalion had been reorganised into two companies —wandered about the "Lady's Leg" all night, and only found its way back to Aquaduct Road at 2.30 a.m.. Our casualties were 6 killed (including 2/Lt. Done, who had only just joined the Battalion), and 17 wounded; and among many acts of gallantry the stretcher bearers particularly distinguished themselves.

Afterwards the Battalion went back to Albert; but before the end of the month it started to march by Contay, Amplier, Bonnières and Croisette to Fiefs, which was reached on the 30th. The Second Division was now in the 13th Corps (Lieut.-General Congreve, V.C.) and ready to take part in the battle of Arras, which started on Easter Monday, April 8th. On that day the Battalion was at La Thieuloye, where Lt. D. H. Wright was very badly wounded in a bombing accident, and where Padre St. John, who had been with us since Tidworth days, bade us farewell. On the 10th we were at Y Huts near Maroeuil, and after a very hurried reconnaisance went forward the next day to take over from the 1/6th Gordon Highlanders the old German front and support lines. Two days later we were on the edge of the high ground, in old German gun-pits, looking across the railway below us to Bailleul, a smoking ruin, and beyond that the great plain of Douai, whose towers were visible on the horizon. A wonderful sight on a clear spring morning, this panorama of a battle field, in which one could actually watch small patrols (of the 23 Royal Fusiliers) feeling their way out beyond Bailleul towards the wood a mile and a half beyond. A harmless-looking wood, but behind it was a village, and a little valley running back to the next village behind that. " If I had been asked to choose a spot in the whole German line to defend," said George Lindsay, the Brigade Major, " I would choose Oppy, because on the map it looks almost impregnable. It could only be taken from the flanks." And the poor old 22nd was destined to attack it frontally !

Not at once. We had four days in the line opposite Gavrelle, relieving the 1st K.R.R.C., and then a week in rest billets at Bray: then a night's bivouacking at Ecurie, and then a march to the front line opposite Oppy Wood, relieving the 1st Kings, with H.Q. in the railway cutting. During the day time the front line was cleared while the artillery cut the formidable wire entanglements : and on the night of the 27/28th the Battalion went back to Gin Trench and Kleeman Stellung on the crest of the hill to await events, while the 17th Middlesex took over battle positions in the front. Owing to small numbers, B and C Companies amalgamated under Major Gregg, A and C under Capt. T. H. Evans, each Company about 120 strong.

The officers who went into action were :—H.Q., Lt.-Col. Barnett Barker, Major Phythian-Adams, Capt. Stone, Capt. Coad, 2/Lt. E. C. Hudson. Right Company, Major Gregg, Capt. de Wet, Lts. Perraton, Stevenson, Steel and Jeffcoat. Left Company, Capt. T. H. Evans, Lts. Parks, Wardley, Palmer and Saword. Capt. J. E. T. Kelly commanded a carrying party of 1st K.R.R.C., and Lts. H. A. Holmes and J. W. Carr had " stragglers posts." The weather was beautiful, with a morning haze. The following extracts from the Colonel's official report describe the progress of the fight and the difficulties encountered.

" ORDERS.—PRELIMINARIES TO ATTACK.

1. There was a Brigade conference on the impending attack at Brigade Headquarters on April 28th about 3.30 p.m. I did not reach my rear Bn. H.Qs. after the conference till 7.30 p.m.

2. I took down verbal orders pending the written Operation Orders. These were to the effect (a) that my Battalion had to pass the starting point—Maison de la Cote—at about 9 p.m.; (b) I had to take over the sector occupied by the Essex Regiment, and (c) zero would be at 3 a.m.

46

3. As my Company H.Qs. in the rear area were somewhat scattered it took some time to collect my Officers. I had sufficient time, however, to make them thoroughly acquainted with all details of the attack. I attach (No. 1) a copy of the Battalion Operation Orders—time did not allow any detailed orders.

4. Fortunately I had kept my men in battle order for the last 10 days, viz. : each man carrying 3 bombs, sandbags and filled water bottle, but owing to some misunderstanding with Brigade Transport about rations, I was unable to obtain the next day's rations. The men left, therefore, with only emergency rations and water in bottles.

5. The men had just done three days in the front line and had only reached their rear positions at 4.30 a.m. that morning. They were, therefore, tired.

6. They passed the starting point almost at the time ordered, and reached their battle positions at 2 a.m.

7. A schedule as to where I might find dumps and their contents was given me by Brigade. Only one dump was within reach. On arrival at my battle H.Qs. an N.C.O. was sent to examine the contents of this dump. It was found mostly blown up and so contained no water and a few boxes of bombs and 5 boxes of S.A.A.

8. Fifty men of the 1st K.R.R.C. who had been carrying the night and day before for the 6th Brigade were given me to act as carriers. I left these men behind at my rear Battalion H.Qs. to bring up rations—they apparently lost their way and did not appear on the scene again until 3 p.m. the next day.

9. Fifty men of the 1st K.R.R.C. (who had also been carrying for the 6th Brigade) were attached to me to form a defensive flank on my right, as no touch had been made with the 63rd Division for 4 days and their exact position was not known.

SITUATION ON ARRIVAL AT BATTLE HEADQUARTERS.

1. I received about 10.15 p.m. a message stating that zero would be at 4 a.m. and not 3 a.m. I at once despatched runners to my Company Commanders. This message reached them as they were forming up in battle position.

2. On arrival at my battle H.Qs. at 3 a.m. Lieut.-Col. Martin, Essex Regiment, informed me (a) that there were no bombs, tools, S.A.A., etc., in any of the trenches; (b) that the

47

dump at Railway Truck had been heavily called on the day previous; and (c) that the German wire on the front of the sector I had to attack was badly cut and in fact not cut at all on the portion facing my Right Company. On the receipt of this information, I at once informed Brigade H.Qs. and my two Company Commanders (see R.B.B. 22, 23, 24 (1) (2) (3).) I made suggestions to the Company Commanders as to how to meet the difficulty and to confer together if time allowed.

THE ATTACK.

(1) As my Battalion was only of the strength of two companies, they were formed up in waves, covering whole front, with 50 men of the 1st K.R.R.C. on right to form a defensive flank. A Company of 23 Royal Fusiliers was given me as a reserve to share with 1st Royal Berks. This was placed at our Battle H.Qs.

(2) The waves were formed up in perfect order and went forward directly the barrage opened, led by the subaltern officers. They were at once hung up by the wire in the dark. By the time gaps had been found, the barrage had lifted off the German trenches. They were thus left exposed to rifle and machine gun fire, and also bombs while looking for gaps and endeavouring to cut the wire. I will now describe the movements of the Right Company (B) throughout the fight and then describe the movements of the Left Company (D Company).

(3) B Company managed with difficulty to get through the first row of German wire. By the time they reached the second row, the barrage had lifted—the second row was found impenetrable. 2/Lt. J. Steele had the whole of his platoon shot down and he and one man managed to get into a shell hole in the wire and remained there all day. Major R. H. Gregg and all other officers except 2/Lt. Jeffcoat became casualties together with most of the men. 2/Lt. Jeffcoat and A/C.S.M. Hogan managed to find a gap on the extreme right. They, with a platoon, jumped into the German Line and captured it with a few prisoners. 2/Lt. Jeffcoat bombed down to the right to try and get in touch with the 63rd Division. A/C.S.M. Hogan bombed up to left to try and get in touch with my D Company. The fighting was very desperate and 2/Lt. Jeffcoat informed me that no quarter was asked or given and many Germans were killed. He succeeded in bombing down to within a point 100 yards of the railway (viz : 400 yards outside Divisional area.) There he obtained touch with the Bedford Regiment. A/C.S.M. Hogan meanwhile worked up about 100 yards to the left. There he established a

48

block. Word was brought to him that 2/Lt. Jeffcoat was in trouble, dealing with a heavy counter attack, so he went down to assist him. On his return to the left, he found it had also been heavily attacked and driven in. All the bombs having been exhausted, the survivors, about 15 in number, had retired to the O.B.L. He at once went after them and organised them for an immediate counter attack. He also wrote me a message describing the situation. 2/Lt. Jeffcoat, finding his rear (left) unprotected, placed a stop, and sent a message to me, giving me the situation.

4. *Left Company (D)*. The right platoon of this Company found the wire uncut and so were all shot, 2/Lt. Palmer, V.C., being the only survivor. He found a shell hole in the wire in which he lay all day. Platoons 14 and 15 appear to have suffered a similar fate and 2/Lt. Parks found himself against impenetrable wire with only 3 Lewis gunners. He therefore retired to O.B.L. and took up a position there. No. 13 Platoon side slipped to the left and got into German Trench. They bombed up to right and left, meeting with heavy opposition—on right they formed a block—on left they joined up with Royal Berks. I left this platoon under Lieut.-Col. Harris, D.S.O., Royal Berks., and they shared the fortunes of the Royal Berks.

5. The 50 men of the 1st K.R.R.C. dug a defensive flank of posts on right flank and garrisoned it. Parties of them got intermingled with the front line fighters and were of the greatest assistance.

6. I am of opinion that the men who had established themselves in the German Line could have maintained their position there till I could reinforce them if proper dumps had been formed and all administrative arrangements been made in perfect order previous to the attack—they only carried three bombs each and the ordinary supply for bombers. The fighting was of a desperate character and the bombs quickly gave out. The Lewis gunners crawled out of the trench and used their guns as sprays and were shot accordingly.

7. Owing to all Officers becoming casualties, I could get no information from the front line at 6 a.m. I sent up my intelligence officer—2/Lt. Hudson—to report on situation. He sent back word at once, and also that bombs must be sent up—he himself became a casualty—the message reached me at 7 a.m. I at once sent up half a company 23rd Royal Fusiliers under Capt. Taylor with orders to garrison O.B.L. and take the situa-

49

tion in hand. I sent with him all the bombs I could find. On arrival at O.B.L. he was in time to prevent A/C.S.M. Hogan wasting men's lives by making a fruitless counter-attack across "No Man's Land." He reported to me at once on the situation as far as he could ascertain it. I sent him S.10 (4). Feeling anxious about the O.B.L., I sent up Capt. Taylor one platoon of 23rd Royal Fusiliers and a Lewis gun.

8. At 9.15 a.m. Col. Harris informed me that the 1st Royal Berks and my platoon were driven back to O.B.L.

9. At 9.20 a.m. I received a message from 2/Lt. Jeffcoat stating that (a) he was in touch with Bedfords; (b) that I could dribble men up to him via the railway; and (c) that if I sent him reinforcements and plenty of bombs, he could attack again and probably capture the line.

*   *   *   *   *   *

12. At 10 a.m. Capt. Bowyer and about 100 men of the 23rd Royal Fusiliers, well supplied with bombs, which had in meanwhile been sent me by the 99th Infantry Brigade, started up the railway. They reached the German line with practically no casualties. Capt. Bowyer at once started operations and he bombed up trench in following order: 23 Royal Fusiliers, 63rd Division, consisting of 7th Battalion Royal Fusiliers, Bedfords, H.A.C. The operation was entirely successful and he established himself firmly at B.18d.4.7., viz., about 200 yards south of Oppy Wood. He did not proceed past this point, although convinced that he could do so, as he thought the Berks might be bombing down to meet him. Also fearing strong counter-attack he wished to keep a large supply of bombs. In the meanwhile, I sent up to him every bomb I could lay my hands on, and also several boxes to Capt. Taylor in the O.B.L. to get across No Man's Land to him. The supply now arriving from 99th Infantry Brigade was ample. Also water and S.A.A. arrived, both of which were badly needed.

13. At about 10.25 a.m. the O.C. Bedfords arrived at my Battalion H.Qs. and gave me the situation on the left. This coincided exactly with 2/Lt. Jeffcoat's report. He agreed to work everything in conjunction with me and we worked most harmoniously together.

14. At 10.25 a.m. Lt.-Col. Harris informed me that a report (unreliable) had reached him that the Germans were attacking in force against the O.B.L. and might drive a gap between 1st Royal Berks and my left. I therefore kept back

six Lewis guns of 23rd Royal Fusiliers and one platoon and also phoned 99th Infantry Brigade to ask for reinforcements. This report was afterwards found to be false. Capt. Taylor, 23rd Royal Fusiliers in O.B.L., during the morning sent his patrols across No Man's Land and kept in touch with Capt. Bowyer's attack. The information he sent me was of the greatest value and his patrols must have acted with great gallantry, as the O.B.L. and No Man's Land were swept with machine gun and rifle fire from Oppy Wood.

15. At 3.15 p.m. the 99th Infantry Brigade informed me that Oppy Wood and Village were reported to be in process of evacuation by enemy. I at once sent out to Capts. Bowyer and Taylor by R.B.B. 30 and 31.

16. I asked O.C. Bedfords to come to my H.Qs. (as previously agreed) to confer.

We agreed that he should push out patrols to practice trenches (B. 13 C and D) and keep touch with my right and in the event of being able to advance that he should capture practice trenches. We also sent for Brigade Machine Gun Officer and instructed him to train his guns on practice ground and sweep approaches south of the village.

17. I then telephoned to Brigade what my future arrangements would be, which were entirely dependent on patrol reports. They were (a) that Capts. Bowyer and Taylor would push on with their remnants of troops and occupy any good positions south and east of village; (b) that I would push up the East Yorks. behind and in support of them; and (c) when touch was once more obtained with enemy, I would relieve them with East Yorks. and draw them back into reserve.

18. At 8.30 p.m. I received a patrol report from Capt. Bowyer to the effect (a) that enemy were holding a trench just west of the sunken road; (b) that there were several hostile posts protected by wire. He added that the trench seemed to be a communication trench running in a half circle starting from Oppy Line and joining up at sunken road. (c) The Oppy Wood patrol reported "enemy still in occupation, about 200 of them being seen proceeding from sunken road to wood."

19. It was reported to me during the day that our second objective did not exist as it had been obliterated by our artillery.

20. I am of opinion (a) that our failure to take the first objective in the first place was simply owing to the wire not being cut and the difficulty in finding the few gaps in the dark.

(b) That in spite of above, men of the 22nd Royal Fusiliers who got into first objective, would have cleared it and maintained themselves there if bombs had been available. The fight was simply a bombing fight as it was in trenches—rifle fire and bayonets were useless.

(c) The supply of bombs and S.A.A. when once they began to arrive from 99th Infantry Brigade was ample, and that had more time been allowed us to properly organise dumps and carrying parties, the attack could not have failed.

(d) The enemy were Guardsmen and fought magnificently. The losses on both sides were therefore about equal.

(e) Their counter-attackers appeared to be splendidly trained and organised and had unlimited bombs.

(f) Our barrage of 6 minutes did not allow sufficient time for men to advance over 150 yards and get through two belts of wire. The barrage had lifted before our men reached the second belt.

*　　*　　*　　*　　*　　*

21. I wish to place on record the splendid gallantry of 2/Lt. Jeffcoat (mortally wounded.) It was entirely owing to the excellent report he sent me on the situation that I was able to push up the 23rd Royal Fusiliers and so capture practically the whole of the objective given me.

The O.C. Bedford Regiment gave me most excellent advice and assistance and our co-operation together was everything that could be desired.

I cannot speak too highly of the most valuable services of Capt. Bowyer and Capt. Taylor, 23rd Royal Fusiliers. The success of our counter-attack and the gaining of our objectives was greatly due to their excellent leadership and gallantry. The information they gave me placed me in a position to give them the assistance they required. It would be impossible to say enough about all the Officers and men of the 23rd Royal Fusiliers who came under my command. They were ready, eager and prepared to move at a moment's notice, quickly understood their orders and carried them out to perfection."

*　　*　　*　　*　　*　　*

So the fight ended, and the Colonel with his 40 men went back to the Railway Cutting through an area drenched with poison gas; sick at heart for the old Regiment that he loved—those who were lying dead in the German wire and those who were lying

52

out wounded on the poisoned ground. But the 22nd was not the only crippled Battalion. The whole Division was in the same state, and yet the fighting had to be continued. The next day more survivors turned up and at last it was just possible to muster a company of 100 men under Lt. Palmer to form part of a composite Battalion, which went to the north side of Oppy Wood and was engaged in a more or less ineffectual attack on the morning of May 3rd. There were 24 casualties, of whom 6 were killed and 6 missing: the remnant rejoined headquarters at Ecoivres on the 6th. A short rest at Beugin, near Ourton, was followed by a fortnight at Ecurie for training and for working parties on the roads; the fine weather broke on the 14th, and the nights were made unpleasant by bombing aeroplanes. Next came a tour of the trenches north of Oppy Wood, during which Capt. Murray was very nearly captured by a German patrol: then we went into close support, with Orchard Dugout, of sultry memory, for H.Q.; after a few days' rest at St. Aubin, more trench life in the Arleux Loop—with some fine patrol work—and back at last to Bray on June 14th.

It is hard to recall the condition of the Battalion. There were 16 trained bombers instead of the 480 that left Yvrench in January. Everyone was sick of fighting, craving for a real rest. And at last Fortune smiled and sent the Battalion on the 20th in busses to the Ecole des Jeunes Filles at Bethune! This was indeed a happy inspiration on someone's part; and instead of the snow and mud of Christmas, 1915, we found beautiful green fields, with grass growing in nearly all the shell holes : duck-boarded trenches and a peaceful enemy. In this delightful neighbourhood the Battalion spent the rest of the summer. Needless to say, as soon as the 2nd Divisional Artillery arrived the pacific indolence of the warfare began to change to a certain alertness : the gas merchants, or Special Company R.E., were never tired of invading our trenches in order to sicken Fritz with some new devilry of gas or liquid fire; and every now and then we made futile attempts to capture Germans. There was Lt. Feord with his Bangalore torpedo; there was Lt. Davies, the prince of patrol leaders; there was Lt. Kiteley and others who went across to the German trenches in broad daylight and brought back souvenirs. But they seldom or never found anyone at home, not even a caretaker; and except for one or two Alsatian deserters we took no prisoners. So tolerable was trench life that tours were prolonged from four to six days, which meant 12 days on end out of the line, and there was leisure to enjoy the summer days mildly at Beuvry or

Noyelles or Bethune. In October the Battalion went right back to Raimbert, a mining village, for a month's intensive training—no doubt in preparation for a fight; but still the numbers were not made up, and there were only about 220 fighting men in the companies. In fact when the Second Division moved in October to the country behind the Passchendaele Ridge, the 22nd were still 200 below strength. Billets were at Herzeele, a pleasant but damp village, where training was almost impossible. Instead, there were rumours—chiefly of Italy, sometimes of the Ridge. And in the middle of it, Col. Barker was suddenly whisked away to command the 3rd Infantry Brigade. His belated promotion—he had been recommended for a Brigade nearly two years—made him very sad; the wrench was too great, the allurements too flimsy. But there was no time to be lost. Red tabs were sewn on to his tunic, and he went away in a motor car stacked high with his kit : and left messages for the officers and for the men whom he, for the first time in his life, hesitated to face. His words need no comment; they are eloquent of the gallant loving-kindness of that great leader of men.

COLONEL BARKER'S FAREWELL MESSAGE.

"On reliquishing Command of the Battalion I wish to place on record my great appreciation and grateful thanks to all ranks for their unswerving loyalty to me at all times.

I was with the the Battalion at its foundation and, in fact, enlisted the first man, and it was my wish to remain with you to the finish—but apparently this cannot be.

You were well thought of at home, quickly made a name for the Battalion in France, and in the fighting line you cannot be surpassed. This is the opinion of not only your near Commanders, but also of the highest. If proof were required (which it is not) our casualties would shew that the 22nd, when needs be, can die to a man. You all feel as I do what we owe to our gallant comrades who gave their lives not only for their Country but for the glory of the Regiment. They have made the Regiment famous and I am absolutely confident that you can only add fresh laurels to our already glorious record.

It was my one ambition to make and keep you a happy Regiment, and if I have succeeded in just one item, I shall feel that I have commanded you successfully.

My parting words to you all are, to keep happy and endeavour to make each other merry and bright. Don't forget that we are all comrades in this great adventure, and that our job is to strafe Germans and not each other. An unhappy man can't fight, and if a Regiment is full of imaginary grievances its fighting spirit disappears.

I hand over the Regiment to Colonel Phythian-Adams with the feeling of the greatest confidence. He has been born and bred a 22nd man, and has proved himself to you on the field of battle. I know that you will extend to him the same confidence and support that you gave to me. He richly deserves the great honour of commanding you and can't be anything but successful.

" Adieu " (I purposely use this word, as " Goodbye " could never be said between us, as long as any of us exist) my brave friends and comrades. May the God of all battles have you in his safe keeping.

R. BARNETT BARKER."

CHAPTER V.

THE LAST PHASE.

"For me, with sorrow I embrace my fortune—
I have some rights of memory."

The promotion of Colonel Barker to a Brigade left a great blank in the Battalion, but the remembrance of his example never failed to illuminate its subsequent history : and its *esprit de corps* was happily not dimmed by the appointment of a stranger to command the 22nd. The mantle fell upon Major Phythian-Adams, the only officer who had been with the Battalion ever since the White City days, who owed all that he knew of leadership to his Colonel; and his only aim during the next three months was to act in every circumstance as " B. B." would have wished. Moreover there was the beloved General Kellett still commanding the Brigade and always keeping a fatherly eye on " the boys." On the anniversary of our landing in France the following messages were exchanged :—" Congratulations from his old and surviving comrades of the 22nd (Service) Battalion, Royal Fusiliers, to their brave and beloved General, who has led them with such success and gallantry for the last two years." " My warmest thanks to my old comrades of the 22nd Royal Fusiliers for their very kind messages which I most deeply appreciate. In the two years of War that we have passed through together you have won for yourselves and the Brigade a magnificent name for fighting and work. I am *very* proud *and* happy to be still with you notwithstanding the ravages of Anno Domini which are leaving their marks heavily upon me. My best wishes to you all for the future. Ever yours, R. O. Kellett."

Events moved rapidly. Five days after B. B.'s departure the Battalion entrained at Esquelbecq in the middle of the night, and instead of going to Italy found itself deposited at Achiet-le-Grand in the afternoon, with the prospect of a ten mile march to Barastre—a terribly trying march at the end of a long day. The first surprise of the Cambrai attack was over, and the Second Division was sent to reinforce the exhausted troops of the 4th Corps. On November 26th, 1917, after a night near Beaumetz, the Battalion took over a bit of the Hindenburg line north of the Cambrai-Bapaume road, in a snow storm. Hardly was this done when it was detached from the Brigade and sent to help General Bradford's Brigade (the 186th), in Bourlon Wood. Who will forget the march in single file along the main road to Anneux, the chalet in the Wood, the dismounted cavalrymen whom we were supporting, the scattered groups breakfasting among the trees, the still more scattered groups when the barrage came down, the disabled tanks, the dead Boches? It was a nightmare of bewilderment and humour and discomfort, so that everyone was thankful to escape from it after two nights and to trudge back to some old trenches on the Hermies-Graincourt road. The casualties had been three officers wounded, other ranks 7 killed, 34 wounded; the Battalion had had an experience not shared by any other unit of the 2nd Division; but unfortunately the result was that when the great German counter-attack opened on November 30th, we were not with our Brigade, and our place was taken by the 17th R. Fusiliers, while we were bandied about from pillar to post throughout the battle. When one reads the brilliant account of the fighting written by Major Wilson (G.S.O. 2) and distributed through the Army, and when one thrills at the story of the magnificent resistance put up by our sister battalion, one cannot help wondering whether the 22nd, in its place, would have achieved an even nobler glory. At any rate the 22nd did all that was required of it, ungrudgingly; and Colonel Phythian-Adams has declared that '' our part was not a minor one. We had the hardest task of any, to manœuvre under another command after days of shelling and fatigue, from which our comrades were exempt, to move here or there, wherever we were most wanted, and finally, when endurance seemed no longer possible, to enter the front line and, at the eleventh hour, to come to grips with the enemy.''

The battle began at 8.45 a.m. on November 30th, and all the morning—a warm fine day when the mist lifted—we heard the roar of it and watched the aeroplanes fighting and the artillery waggons being driven at a gallop through the hostile barrage in front of us. But at last it was our turn to face that barrage, and the Battalion moved off at 1.30 p.m. by companies and managed to reach the old Hindenburg front line near Lock 6 on the Canal du Nord with only 7 casualties. Here were batteries of our field guns; and the sight of young Quiller-Couch dancing for joy at the finest day's shoot he had ever had put great heart into all who saw him. The fight was going well; the field guns were firing over open sights, the machine guns and Lewis guns had such targets as had been hitherto regarded as impracticable dreams, and the only posts which had been driven in on the extreme right had been recovered by the 23rd Royal Fusiliers. As for the 22nd, it was under command of the 5th Infantry Brigade for 24 hours on the left bank of the Canal, employed in supporting the 17th Middlesex, who were being hard pressed from the direction of Moeuvres. On the evening of the 1st it was transferred to the 6th Infantry Brigade and went to relieve the 13th Essex in Canal Trench and Kangaroo Trench, with the responsibility for defending the Canal itself as well. This was one of the nastiest positions ever held by the Battalion. Canal Trench was nothing but a sap 300 yards long with a block at the end of it beyond which was a German redoubt with a dug-out capable of holding 300 men. The trench was entirely exposed on both flanks—there was not a scrap of wire—and ran parallel to the Canal bank back to the main road behind which were the supports in Kangaroo Trench. A German counter-attack was expected on the 2nd. However, every effort was made to consolidate. Some wire was put out so as to deflect any advancing enemy towards our Lewis guns posted in a transverse trench; and the "tump-line platoon" stocked the line with no less than 200 boxes of bombs and S.A.A. during the night. All day long during the 2nd the enemy were reported to be concentrating, and at 4.45 p.m. the S.O.S. rocket went up along the whole Divisional front. Presently two parties of Germans, each about 30 strong, jumped out of their strong post and came down either side of Canal Trench, keeping their distance and throwing bombs into it; but the response was electric, our Lewis guns discomfited them and after half an hour's brisk firing and bombing the survivors vanished back to their trench. We had only 15 casualties. The night was spent in making T-heads along Canal Trench, wiring and patrolling. The next morning heavy shelling on the Cambrai road and Battalion H.Q. severed all communications, but no attack followed : at noon the G.O.C. 5th Infantry Brigade took over command of the Battalion again : at 4.30 p.m. the enemy had another go at our sap-head but was more easily driven back; and during the night further progress was made in consolidating and wiring the positions, while a patrol ventured 300 yards up the bed of the Canal and located the enemy's forward machine gun positions. But all the labour of consolidation was wasted, for at noon on the 4th orders arrived that the line was to be " readjusted " and troops withdrawn. This was quite a new experience for the 22nd, but was undertaken with skill and cheerfulness. After dark the companies retired, leaving only a small rear guard with a couple of Lewis guns to blow in dug-outs and, by constant firing, to prevent the Germans from discovering the withdrawal. This was successfully done : by dawn everyone was safely back in the new line, except, it is said, one man who was left behind by mistake and who came back at the double in broad daylight with the enemy in full cry. Our total casualties were under 20 per cent. The officers who went into this action were :—H.Q., Lt.-Col. Phythian-Adams, Major Stone, Lt. Bexon; Capt. Neilson, R.A.M.C.; Lt. Bird and Lt. Fisher (tump-line platoon) : A. Company, Lts. Andrew, Wolf, Coppack, Freston; B Company, Capt. Goodman, Lts. H. A. Holmes, Abbott, Park and Brownlee; C Company, Capt. W. A. Murray, Lts. Talbot, Pargeter, Franklin, Myles and Vaughan; D Company, Lts. Carr, Hope and Lloyd.

After a few days rest the Battalion took over the new front at Hughes Switch and found itself for the second time in its wanderings next door to the 22nd London Regiment. Things were fairly lively, but the weather was determined to cool excessive pugnacity. Batt H.Q. being cut off from the front by day, Major Scott was in command of the front line area, and a German bombing attack was successfully demolished by D Company on December 15th. Christmas was spent in the hut camp at Barastre, but Boxing Night found the Battalion back in the front line, the night on which poor L./Cpl. E. J. Rowe was blinded by a shell. The New Year, 1918, began in Brigade reserve at Hermies, followed by nearly three weeks' inactivity in the mud of Barastre; and then came the last tour of the trenches —in a new sector, opposite La Vacquerie, where we took over, from the Howe Battalion R.N.D., ground which the Germans had attacked on November 30th with far more success than at Moeuvres. They were interesting trenches, though not very comfortable, and as usual we set to work to increase the interest and comfort of them, and Sgt. Hawthorne, with a fine piece of patrol work, won the last D.C.M. for the Battalion.

An ironical thing had happened. General Kellett had at last been obliged to give in to "Anno Domini" and to go home for the rest of the war; and General Barker had realised the dream that had haunted him ever since his promotion—he was sent for to command the 99th Infantry Brigade, and arrived at Advanced Brigade H.Q., near Villers Plouich, to find the 22nd within ten minutes' walk of him and under his command again. But the happiness of this reunion was short-lived; for almost his first duty was to break the news to his old Battalion that it was to be disbanded immediately. Under the new scheme of three-battalion Brigades, one battalion of the Fusiliers was doomed, and by the casting of lots the 22nd was chosen by the Corps Commander. When Colonel Phythian-Adams came back from leave on January 30th he was confronted by this decision, and from February 5th, 1918, the Battalion ceased to exist.

There was no use in protesting—though the Mayor of Kensington did all he could to rescind the doom—no use in repining; no use in doing anything but submitting to the inevitable and attempting to smooth matters. The sympathy of the whole Brigade, the whole Division, was with us, as B.B. expressed in his famous farewell.

In bidding farewell to the 22nd Battalion Royal Fusiliers (Kensington) I am sure I voice the feelings of all ranks of the 99th Brigade in expressing our deep regret that we have to part with such comrades.

Since November 1915, under the able leadership of our beloved and gallant brigadier, Brigadier-General R. O. KELLETT, C.B., C.M.G., we have fought together in the following actions :—Delville Wood, Vimy Ridge, The Ancre, Miraumont, Grevillers Trench, Oppy and Cambrai, in every one of which the 22nd Royal Fusiliers played a conspicuous part.

The mention of these important actions, in which we have added fame to the 2nd Division, is sufficient to prove the magnificent part you have filled in making the History of the 99th Brigade.

We all understand with what feelings you must view the disbanding of your fine battalion. We know full well, your splendid *esprit de corps* which engendered your fine fighting spirit.

We know of the N.C.O's. and men, still with you, who gave up their all in 1914 to join you. Nor do we forget your many heroes who died for you and us all.

Knowing full well all this, we can truly offer you our heartfelt sympathies in your day of trial.

The 22nd Battalion Royal Fusiliers never lost a yard of trench or failed their comrades in the day of battle. Such is your record and such a record of you will be handed down to posterity.

All of you, I am thankful to say will remain in our famous Division and 300 of you in the old Brigade.

I know that the 22nd Royal Fusiliers will accept the inevitable in their usual fine spirit, and will in time transfer the *esprit de corps* they always prized so dearly, to their sister battalions.

I feel certain their sister battalions will welcome them with open arms and endeavour to heal the sores you now so intensely feel.

As one who served with you from the day of your foundation to your disbandment (except for 2 months) I know full well what this step means to you all.

I also know that, though the 22nd Battalion Royal Fusiliers has ceased to exist as a Unit, you will not forget that we are all Englishmen fighting Germans, and that the fine indomitable spirit of the Battalion will still carry you on until the One Red and Two White Stars are inscribed on the Forts of the Rhine.

R. BARNETT BARKER,

Brigadier General,

2/2/1918.   Commanding 99th Infantry Brigade.

In a private letter on February 3rd he wrote, " On calmly considering things, I am not so sad as I was. If anything had happened to ——————— or ——————— the dear old Regiment would have drifted into strange hands and anything might have happened to them. They finish their glorious career at the top of their form. They have never failed to take their objective or lost a yard of trench. They have also taken part in the heaviest fighting of the whole war, and have readily sacrificed themselves, as at Oppy, when necessary."

There were some feverish melancholy days at Metz-en-Couture, spent in organising the disbandment. Fifteen officers and 309 other ranks, including nearly all the original " K's " of the Battalion, went to the 23rd Royal Fusiliers and were received with the utmost consideration; fourteen officers and 274 other ranks to the 24th Royal Fusiliers. The General spared no effort to " wangle " as many of his veterans as possible into Brigade Headquarters; and every N.C.O. or man who wished to take a Commission was recommended. The Colonel eventually went to the 1st Army School as instructor, and Major Stone was privileged to follow General Barker till that gallant and glorious life was snuffed out by a stray shell on March 24th in the ghastly retreat.

So ended the history of the 22nd Royal Fusiliers, abruptly, in the twinkling of an eye, within nine months of the end of the war. Of the men who lived to fight in other Battalions, of their deeds, of the traditions that they upheld, the honours that they won, the fortunes of wound or prison life or death that they encountered, who shall tell ? Only we know that for us the great days were over with the passing of the 22nd; that whether we " retired from the war " or carried on in new surroundings with a dismal loyalty to the broader *esprit de corps,* we should never recapture the glories of the old comradeship, never find elsewhere the love of our devoted leader. And now, when all is over, with our Colours hanging in Kensington Town Hall, with the Old Comrades Association struggling to carry out the duties that we all owe to one another, with *Mufti* also struggling—alas !—to keep communications open between H.Q. and the furthest outposts, it is still but the afterglow of a sun that has set, the echo of a voice that is for ever silenced.

CHAPTER VI.

MISCELLANIES.

It would be a pity to close the foregoing bald narrative of the Battalion's doings without some disjointed notes on the various matters which have hitherto been omitted. Statistics compiled from War Diaries are not always to be trusted; but it appears that whereas the 22nd landed in France with 30 officers in 1915, and had 33 at the moment of disbandment, it lost 90 by death, wounds, illness or other causes, not counting those like Capt. W. A. Murray, M.C., who went and returned again. Capt. Murray, by the way, was the first officer wounded; he came back just in time for Delville Wood, where he was wounded again, and disappeared for nearly a year. He came again just after Oppy, was given a Company, and almost instantly had an encounter with a German patrol, who wounded him and carried him away, till he struggled loose, and fell into an old trench, whence he was rescued. Nothing daunted, he reappeared from hospital in time to command C Company again in the Cambrai fighting, and was wounded for the fourth time, and on this occasion very badly wounded, in Canal Trench, on December 2nd, 1917.

The figures for " other ranks " are similar, showing a wastage of about 2,230 men between November, 1915, and February, 1918; so that roughly every officer who landed in France was replaced three times, and every other rank two-and-a-quarter times; or, in other words, an officer lasted for nine months, an other rank for a year on the average.

Naturally it was on Headquarters and in the Transport lines that the majority of the " K " men or veterans of the White City were found at the end. In France, the successive R.S.M.'s were F. J. Smith, R. D. Burgess, F. Stevens, W. A. Rumble, a very distinguished quartet who are all alive to-day. Smith became Quartermaster when Lt. Merrell went home, and in turn when he was invalided home he was succeeded by R. D. Burgess, who was responsible for the Q.M. Stores till the end. The Battalion was better supplied with clothing, and probably, too, was better fed than any other Battalion in the Army! In the trenches every night either the Q.M. and the transport sergeant or the transport officer and the R.Q.M. sergeant reported the arrival of rations to Battalion H.Q. The Transport was magnificent. Under Captain Ross and Sergt. Mark Neyland it was the pride of the Brigadier, and its success in the Horse Shows of the summer of 1917 was only the culmination of its unfailing smartness and efficiency. In the Divisional Horse Show at Ecurie on June 12th, the turn-out (1 cooker, 1 water-cart and two G.S. limbers) won by 23 points from the 2nd H.L.I., while a light draught horse not only won there but also at the 13th Corps Show, when the turn-out was just beaten by the D.C.L.I. At one period, during the Oppy fighting, a notable addition was made to the Transport by the mysterious arrival of the pioneer's horse, "Oppy," the narrowest quadruped in the world, which might be seen dragging a truck containing all Sergt. Lindsay's and Sergt. McGowan's paraphernalia. How it appeared, how it fed, how it eventually vanished, was never officially asked or explained, but it is generally agreed that it was not a mortal horse.

The Pioneers and the Sanitary Section were all famous men. The last to leave any camp, they were the first to arrive at the next. Trained to perfection by the C.O., they never failed to make billets into palaces as if by a magic wand; or perhaps one should say H.Q. mess into a palace. The Pioneers' masterpiece was probably the summer headquarters in the trenches at Cambrin, where millions of sandbags were used to upholster the verandah; and there was a night at Givenchy when, Burgess and Lockyear assisting, the H. Q. mess was practically rebuilt before dawn. Famous men, too, were the police, from Sergt. Spillane, who lost his arm, to Theodore Jones, who lost his job, intruding into many a pleasant or hectic memory.

And then the Medical Officers and their Staff! Capt. Miller, D.S.O., M.C., hero of a hundred escapades, who would never allow a case of trench-foot to go to hospital, but had private rest-houses for sick men; and Captain Coad, most urbane of men; Captain Wynter and Captain Neilson. What would any of them have done without their capable assistants, from Sergt Gimson to Sergt. Metcalfe? Without Parkinson of the golden tooth (wounded at Oppy) or L-Corpl. James Steele, timber thief, or "Alice" Hughes?

The Battalion had practically only one Chaplain, Padre St. John, who still keeps up his connection with us through the O.C.A. The memory goes back to many services in France, before battles, after battles, in sheds and barns and huts or in the open-air; services which for their poignancy can never be repeated, nor for their simple and appropriate surroundings. We were very lucky in our Padre, whose sense of humour was as large as his heart.

Much might be written of the Signallers, for their share in the battle honours of the Battalion is almost epical. Practically unofficered all the time, they maintained a standard of efficiency second to no other unit : their bravery and perseverance, their good fellowship, their keenness were displayed by one and all; but they owed their standards chiefly to the leadership of Sergt. Keeble and Corpl. West. And with the Signallers must be joined the Orderlies, for in their work they were complementary, if not always complimentary, to each other. The Orderlies were picked men, the cheerfulest gang imaginable, exchanging their life of leisure out of trenches for one of superhuman endurance and courage in a fight; always cool, always ready, and generally smiling. It is invidious to mention names, but Corpl. Dennis, L.-Corpl. Halstead and Ptes. Wratten and James seemed in their different ways to be typical of the ideal runner.

A word of recognition is due to the Orderly Room Staff also : Sergt. Dicky Bird and Corpl. Munro, the veterans from Tidworth to the end; with Sergt. Turney, who came up to relieve Sergt. Bird in the last phase : an invaluable, overworked staff, struggling cheerfully through the avalanche of memos. and returns week after week—the prop and mainstay of successive adjutants.

It has not been possible in the course of the narrative to notice the various innovations which came gradually; the slow adoption of the steel helmet, the exchange of the P.H. helmet for the box respirator; the interesting development of telephone communications up to the arrival of the Fullerphone; the gradual equipment of battalions with Lewis guns, till at last there was a L.G. section in each platoon; the intensive training of platoons themselves : the use of dummy trenches, or distinguishing badges; the invention of the Mills bomb; the first appearance of the Stokes trench mortar in the Vimy period (and in the Talus des Zouaves, by the way, the French had left a monster mortar, named Bébé, which used to toss a shell as big as a man on to the Ridge, a delightful spectacle for all except those in the deep field); the two-inch trench mortars in the Ancre fight and their wasted ammunition; the evolution of the Brigade Machine Gun Companies. Nor has it been possible to do justice to the records of patrolling or wiring or raiding. But there are two things which deserve a mention at all costs. One was the Hebuterne raid of September 15th, 1916, which was for a long times regarded as an example of how a raid should be conducted. It was the first time that a box barrage was used. At 10.35 p.m. the raiding part, 2/Lt. W. J. R. Martin and 25 other ranks, mostly armed with revolvers, bombs or clubs, began to crawl across No Man's Land while the artillery put a barrage all along that part of the German front line. At 10.45 the barrage lifted off the sap and bit of trench that were to be entered, and descended again in the shape of three sides of a square, cutting off the doomed inhabitants from retreat or help. At the same moment, six Stokes mortars which had been installed in our front line deluged the chosen spot with concentrated rapid fire for one minute, at the end of which the raiding party, split up into three sections, ran forward and jumped into the sap and the trench. So thorough had been the preparation that very little resistance was encountered : a German officer and eleven men were killed, ten live Germans were made to accompany the raiders back, and everyone got safely to our Battalion H.Q. without a scratch. The completeness of the success was largely due to the machine guns, which kept all German heads down under cover during the period of the raid and the return, as well as to the co-operation of artillery and T.M. Battery; but it was also due to the fact that the raiders meant business throughout. What share Doc. Miller and his stretcher-bearers had in the raid it would be impolitic to guess, but the regulations of the Geneva Convention were seriously imperilled that night !

The other thing to be mentioned is the Tump-line Platoon, which was instituted at Raimbert in the autumn of 1917 after experiments with Yukon packs and Tump-lines to meet the necessity of supplying fighting troops with more ammunition than they could carry themselves. In all fights carrying parties had been specially detailed for this purpose; but obviously it would be more economical and effective to *train* certain men who were not suitable for actual fighting in the art of carrying scientifically and methodically. The result of the experiment was amazing. 2/Lt. Fisher and his Tump-liners proved in the Cambrai fight that they could supply forward troops with S.A.A. bombs, water, or rations with far more speed and reliability than any scratch carrying party; and, what is more, the Tump-liners, mostly oldish men who had not great combative value, began to display a great *esprit de corps,* and very soon it was difficult to stop them from carrying everything that they could lay hands on to the front line. They worried the Staff Captains who were responsible for the Brigade dumps !

Economy of material was a great cry towards the end of the war, and the competitive system of valuing whatever stuff Battalions brought to Salvage Dumps produced great results. The ration carts generally went back from the trenches laden with old rifles, shell cases, and equipment for the return journey, and in 1917 the amount credited to the 22nd for salvage was no less than £3,013, a fine record.

No history of the Battalion would be complete without some reference to the spirit of comradeship which survived the winter of separation and blossomed again in the spring of demobilisation. The idea germinated in Kensington after the Armistice, but it was not till the Peace Celebrations in July, 1919, that it budded in a meeting at the Kensington Town Hall, under the chairmanship of Major Gregg, in the absence of Col. Phythian-Adams, who has relapsed into his pre-war habits by joining the British School of Archæology in Jerusalem. At this first meeting an Old Comrades' Association was formed, and the following message of condolence passed for distribution among the next-of-kin of all our fallen comrades :

We, the first General Meeting of the survivors of the 22nd (Kensington) Battalion the Royal Fusiliers, wish to express to you, the relatives of our comrade who gave his life for our King and Country, the deep and unfailing honour in which we hold his memory. We, who knew something of the daily hazard of life on the Western Front—how one man is taken and the other left, how death may come in an instant or after hours of suffering ; we, who are proud of our battalion and of the spirit that animated it throughout its history, wish to place on record at this first opportunity our gratitude to our fallen comrades for the example and the inspiration that they gave us in their lives and by their deaths. And we pray for you, who waited in suspense and at the end heard the grievous tidings from across the sea, that God may comfort you in your loss, and that pride in the record of our battalion may temper the bitterness of your sorrow. July 26th, 1919.

Sir William Davison accepted the presidency of the new Association, and with the assistance of a strong Committee, mostly of Londoners, entered with enthusiasm into the work of re-establishing connection between the far-scattered members of the Battalion, of keeping the spirit of comradeship alive and of helping those who needed help. A Committee Room was established at 156, Ladbroke Grove, through the generosity of friends, and a magazine called " Mufti " was started; annual dinners with an average attendance of about 100, whist drives, concerts, sports, and even children's parties have been organized by the indefatigable Committee, and against formidable financial difficulties a really wonderful amount of practical and steadfast work has been done, for which the thanks of every member of the Battalion are due. This Record owes its inception to the O.C.A. and must be regarded as only supplementary to the entertaining pages of " Mufti," which abound in lively reminiscences of the great days. It is unnecessary to mention names, but the list of officers of the Association on the last page of this volume contains most of those whose loyalty to the traditions and honour of the Battalion has been proved and proved again.

A subscription list for War Memorial Funds in " Mufti " produced over £50 and was distributed between the 2nd Division War Memorial at Moeuvres (designed by Major J. B. Scott and due to be dedicated at Whitsuntide, 1923), the Horsham War Memorial in the Carfax, and the Kensington War Memorial. Two memorial services have been held at Horsham, and wreaths laid upon the Memorial in the presence of huge concourses of our old friends in the town. The Kensington Memorial has this inscription on the side :—

" The 22nd (Kensington) Battalion, Royal Fusiliers, City of London Regiment. Battle record—Vimy Ridge, Delville Wood, Guillemont, The Somme, 1916, Beaumont Hamel, Serre, The Ancre, Grevillers, Miraumont, Oppy Wood, Bourlon Wood, Cambrai."

A proud record this, which we share with the 13th Londons ! And with them, too, we share memories of Souchez, which has been " adopted " by the Royal Borough. Our colours, which we did not receive till after the war, are hanging in the Town Hall at Kensington, an abiding memory of the Battalion which served the Borough so well. The Royal Fusiliers Memorial at Holborn Bars was unveiled on November 4th, 1922, and the 22nd Royal Fusiliers also receives its share of recognition in two war histories at least—*The History of the 2nd Division*, by Everard Wyrall, and *The History of the Royal Fusiliers*, 1914-1918, by Major H. C. O'Neill.

Thus on a note of sombre reminiscence this short Record must end. Readers, as well as writer, must be thinking, " If only B.B. had lived what a difference he would have made to all of us—now—after the war ! How he would have cheered our re-unions, with what unsparing diligence he would have continued to father us, with what indignation he would have righted our wrongs!'' But what has been done in the way of cheerfulness and usefulness has been done in the spirit which he would have approved; and he would certainly have been the first to initiate that testimony of loyalty and affection which Major Scott illuminated and engraved on vellum for the Battalion to send to General Kellett in November, 1919. In acknowledging the '' most gracious and touching message,'' the General wrote, '' I have many things that I value, but there is none in which I shall have more pride than this Address, coming, as it does, from men with whom I had the privilege and honour of being so closely associated throughout nearly three years in the Great War. While I live, the 22nd Royal Fusiliers will always have a space, and a considerable one, in the bottom of my heart.''

So is it with all of us—while we live—in the bottom of our hearts—a precious and fragrant memory of great days, great heroes, great comrades, such as we shall never know again.

EPILOGUE

BY

Lt.-Col. W. J. PHYTHIAN-ADAMS, D.S.O., M.C.

———

The Story of the " 22nd " is told. Its end came in one sense on a wintry day at Metz-en-Couture, when the G. O. C. 2nd Division took leave of the Battalion in a soldierly speech which warmed the hearts and stimulated the courage of all who heard it.

But, perhaps, in another sense it ended more truly (if our later joined comrades will allow me to say this), when the Commanding Officer bade a final farewell to the little group of men who represented the remnants of the White City and Roffey days.

The youth of the 22nd had been strange but happy, its adolescence strenuous but always cheerful, and when the time arrived for Action in the Field, it came to that moment, as it were, in its manhood's prime.

It had a spirit of its own, a peculiar spirit, which other Regiments, without understanding it, recognised and respected, and in its long record of warfare well accomplished, it bore that spirit aloft like a banner and laid it, at the last, untarnished in the Temple where brave deeds are recorded and the Great Sacrifice meets with its reward.

APPENDIX I.

List of Decorations and Awards.

Victoria Cross.

Palmer, F. W.

D.S.O. and Bar.

Barnett Barker, R.

D.S.O.

Phythian-Adams, W. J.   Miller, W. A. (R.A.M.C.)
Gregg, R. H.   Stone, C. R.

M. C.

Phythian-Adams. W. J.   Martin, W. J. R.
Blomfield, A. J.   Miller, W. A.
Burgess, R. W.   Orme, E. R.
Carr, J. W.   Perraton, F. M.
Coad, C. N.   Roscoe, R. L.
Evans, G. H.   Rossell, E. C.
Evans, T. H.   St. John, Revd. E. P.
Feord, A.   Simons, L.
Gell, E. A. S.   Stone, C. R.
Gregg, R. H.

D.C.M.

Baker, F. R.   Keeble, A. T.
Brierly, M. R.   McGowan, T. E.
Carr, J. W.   Metcalfe, W. H.
Evans, G. H.   Miles, F. G.
Fidler, C. E.   Mobley, A.
Fisher, P. W.   Rumble, W. A.
Harvey, H. E.   Robinson, R.
Hawthorne, L.   Webb, G.
Hogan, L. U.   Wheeler, C. A.

M. M. and Bar.

Guy, E. C.

Wilkinson, H. V.

Leonard, J.

M. M.

Ayres, G.
Baldwin, J.
Blundell, T.
Bone, C. C.
Booth, H.
Brown, L.
Burgess, A. F.
Cannot, P. A.
Cole, C.
Crane, E.
Dennis, H. G.
Downing, J. T.
Duke, R.
Fahey, W. J.
Faux, C. Y.
Fitton, J. W.
Garman, V.
Gent, F.
Gimson, S. G.
Griffin, E.
Gullen, J. B. W.
Guyatt, G.
Halstead, H.
Hawes, R.
Harrington, H. V.
Harvey, H. E.
Hennessey, H. W.
Herrington, H.
Hepburn, A. B.
Keeble, A. T.
Kirby, F. D.
Lindsey, C.

McGowan, T. E.
Martin, C.
Martin, R.
Moon, G. J.
Moore, H. J.
Merton, J. T.
Palmer, F. W.
Pearson, C. E.
Peatfield, W.
Petchey, J.
Place, F. C.
Porker, L. H.
Richardson, H.
Rogerson, R. H.
Shoreman, L. E.
Smith, T.
Stroud, A.
Stewart, L. T.
Taylor, E.
Taylor, W. B.
Temple, G. M.
Turner, W.
Vaisey, J. C.
Wagland, P.
Ward, R.
Wharton, W. H.
West, E. M.
White, W. J.
Wilmot, P. E.
Woodward, E.
Wratten, S.

M.S.M.

Turney, C.

Belgian Croix-de-Guerre.

Amery, T. A.

Mentioned in Despatches.

Lieut.-Col. R. B. Barker, D.S.O. (thrice).
Major J. Walsh.
Lieut. J. Ross.
Temp.-Lieut. R. L. Roscoe.
Sergt.-Major R. D. Burgess.
Sergt.-Major G. H. Hartley.
Sergt. M. R. Brierley.
Corpl. W. J. Butcher.
Corpl. H. G. Dennis.

Act of Courage.

Pte. H. W. Woolford.
(Voluntarily supplied 22 fluid ounces of blood for transfusion).

APPENDIX II.

Roll of Honour.

1916.   OFFICERS.

June   1st.   2/Lt. C. J. Fowler [d of w], Vimy Ridge.

June 21st.   Capt. G. D. A. Black [k in a], Vimy Ridge
                                          b Cabaret Rouge.

July 27th.   Capt. C. Grant [k in a], Delville Wood.

Aug.   3rd.   Capt. A. MacDougall [k in a], Delville Wood
                                         b at the Citadel.

Sept. 12th.   2/Lt. P. W. Fisher, D.C.M. [k in a], at Hébuterne.

Nov. 13th.   2/Lt. N. Fitton [k in a], Ancre.

1917.

Feb.   4th.   Capt. R. L. Roscoe, M.C. [d of w], Courcelette,
                                         b at Contay.

Feb. 17th.   Capt. L. Simons, M.C. missing, Miraumont.

Feb. 17th.   2/Lt. J. H. E. Ellison missing, Miraumont.

Feb. 17th.   2/Lt. W. H. Payne [k in a], Miraumont.

Feb. 17th.   2/Lt. E. A. Burgess [k in a], Miraumont.

Feb. 18th.   2/Lt. S. F. Boulter [d of w], Miraumont.

Feb. 19th.   Major J. Walsh, M.C. [d of w], Miraumont
                                         b at Ovillers.

Mar. 10th.   2/Lt. N. S. Done [k in a], Grevillers.

April 29th.   2/Lt. M. E Wardley [k in a] Oppy.

April 29th.   2/Lt. R. Saword, missing, Oppy.

April 29th.   2/Lt. F. M. Perraton, M.C., missing, Oppy.

April 29th.   2/Lt. F. Stevenson, missing, Oppy.

April 29th.   2/Lt. S. F. Jeffcoat [d of w] Oppy.

1918.

Mar. 25th.   Brig.-Gen. R. Barnett Barker, D.S.O., commanding
              99th Inf. Bde. [k in a], Gueudecourt, b at Albert.

WARRANT OFFICERS, N.C.O.'s & MEN.

A Company. 1916.

Vango, T. L.
Monahan, D.
Humphrey, J.
Jones, T.
Murton, A. S.
Baldwin, T. C.
Kellern, H.
Mountier, A. A.
Ashton, A. E. B.
Bascombe, W.
Reid, R. A.
Barnes, W.
Lindsay, A. E.
Such, S.
Stark, F. C.
Harrington, W.
Cotton, C.
Goodhew, J.

Westland, N. G.
Burton, W.
Cane, J. M.
Davies, H.
Gould, J. B.
Levey, J.
Bedwell, R.
Stevens, H. G.
Christian, O. M.
Heath, S. W.
Meyers, E. J.
Kilminster, J. W.
Taylor, J.
Ward, J.
Brown, F. E.
Munro, H. H.
Turner, A. E.

B Company. 1916.

Coombs, W.
Edgington, A. J.
Neale, H. D.
Pescud, A. J.
Laidman, K.
Berry, R. H.
Cook, H. W.
Drew, R.
Pearce, B. S.
Van Tromp, H.
Gardner, L. V.
Stannard, G. M.
Wells, M. G. L.
Greene, F. G.
Kench, S. J.
Guest, A.
Halstead, F. F. R.
Ward, F J.
Dillon, F.
Barden, H.
Hearn, R. P.

Barcham, F.
Markie, J.
Gallop, A.
Hardy, R. W.
Bennett, L.
Lawton, C.
Wharton, H.
Gould, A.
Barwise, L. W.
Scarrold, G. H.
Hennessey, J. M.
Herbert, E.
Corcoran, J.
Hudson, A.
Stewart, J. F.
Corbett, H.
Vickery, A. E.
Bowden, W. J.
Ansell, G. F.
Ginsberg, S.
Janison, P. W. L.

B Company. 1916 (*continued*).

Phœnix, A.
Cohen, D.
Miller, E. H.
Pearce, A.
Mortimer, A. J.
Taylor, G. H.
Booker, G. L.
Russell-Davies, L. G.
Finlayson, R. I.
Andrews, H.
Basnett, J.

Luke, J.
Atherton, T.
Ells, J.
Fidler, J.
Jackson, H.
Pilkington, R. D. S.
White, C. E.
Springall, A. W. G.
Roe, A. J.
Grant, J.
Johnson, G. H.

C Company. 1916.

Smith, F.
Jones, G. A. H.
Farrell, T. W.
Jeffrey, H. A.
Kelly, E. J.
Hedges, A J.
Wilson, W. J.
Judge, G.
Watson, R.
Belton, J.
English, G.
Whitlock, H. E.
Alp, F. H. B.
Youels, H. A.
Weedon, R.
Widdowson, B.
Ayling, G. P.
Steward, W. J.
Farley, R.
Perry, A.
Barnett, A.
Hine, A. C.
Wiles, G.
Negus, J.
Peverill, T.
Clark, C.
Clarke, J.

Davis, F.
Grigg, A. J.
Huggins, T.
Leppard, P.
Pritchard, G.
Wood, H.
Darrington, W.
Mc. Guinness. J.
Dearden, A. J.
Hayes, F. A.
Kessell, F. H.
Levens, J. S.
Banfield, T. S.
Evans, J. E.
Sarsfield, F. P.
Brackenbury, J. H.
Foster, G.
Coplestone, E. A.
Keates, W. M.
Passfield, W.
Lovendahl, W.
Yeoman, J. F.
Phillips, E.
Penn, W.
Taylor, H.
Garman, V.
Randall, W. L.

D Company. 1916.

Morris, C.
Measures, A. E.

Hoare, S. P.
Ashton, J. G. R.

D Company. 1916 (*continued*).

North, W. G. B.
Timms, E. W.
Livingstone, D.
Tong, A. E.
Harding, W. C.
Pyke, C.
Ulph, W.
Dixon, G.
Brown, E. E.
Haddock, W.
Craib, J. E.
Cuthbertson, F.
Escudier, H.
Grover, E. B.
Keen, F. W.
Penwarden, J.
Scott, G. A.

Stacey, R. F. W.
Ransom, J. F.
Winsburg, J.
Edgeller, A. F. C.
Smith, F. W. J.
Stokes, W.
Bailey, S.
Hood, H. C.
Richards, F. W.
Wright, A.
Williams, G. A.
Clark, E. R.
Higgins, A.
Sayers, R.
Gardener, C. H.
Garston, S. H.

A Company. 1917.

Kingsland, F. W.
Tonge, R. S.
Giles, A. T.
Hare, J. P.
Destrubé, C. G.
Barber, H. B.
Blackwell, H.
Ecob, H.
Slade, A. E.
Barttelot, R. W.
Larner, A. J.
Meeds, E. J.
Ross, J. T.
Amor, G. F.
Avery, H.
Barnslade, R.
Destrube, P. J.
Garner, J.

Goulding, P.
Holmes, H. H.
Symonds, W. J.
Ward, L. J.
Copeland, F. A.
Farnes, A.
Powell, H. W.
Bartlett, A. G.
Arnell, E.
Minty, W. E.
Clements, T. G.
Bartlett, R. L.
Finer, H. J.
Price, F.
Outram, A. R.
Milne, J.
Hennessey, H. W.
Easton, H.

B Company. 1917.

Merricks, S.
Brewer, W.
Brierly, M. R.

Archer, J. H.
Bateman, L. R.
Brough, E.

Carrack, C. J.
Carter, R.
Jackson, W. J.
Kirkland, R.
Moxon, G.
Payne, C. R.
Thurston, R.
Tubby, C. G.
Verrall, P. R.
Walters, J. H.
Wiles, F.
Williams, F. F.
Akhurst, A. H.
Hinchsliff, G.
Holden, F.
Robinson, R. L.
Wright, W. P.
Walsh, W.
Green, G. L.
Hore, S. J.
Crondace, H.
Stratton, C. E.
Talkington, W.
Irving, F.
O'Donnell, J.
Barnes, C. J.
Batte, G.
Durber, E.
Gilbert, C.
Lingwood, W. J.
Chandler, J.
Hackett, C. F.
Forecast, C.
Bannerman, J. D.
Bear, H.
Gibson, B.
Morton, A. V.
Hulyer, E. A.
Phillips, A. H. P.
Hay, A. E.
Snell, J. H.
Andrews, H. M.

Petchy, J.
Harding, E. S.
Lowry, H.
Brickell, P. H.
Griffiths, J. F.
Boraston, J. P. S.
Field, H.
Trafford, T. J.
Staples, A. H.
Aston, J. E.
Bonner, H. J.
Wales, W. J.
Spatcher, C. P.
Vassey, W. A.
Shepherd, H. A.
Patching, C.
Page, A. R. P.
Farrimond, T.
Chilvers, F. G.
Webb, A. J.
Wright, S. H.
Frampton, W. J.
Curley, J.
Craft, C.
Rogers, L. A.
Barrow, W.
Blackstock, J.
Rose, J. A.
Hughes, R. V.
Lyon, C. C.
Mash, H.
Corsi, F.
Orders, A.
Fair, C.
Purver, L. A.
Eden, T.
Smith, T.
Gore, A. S.
Smith, W.
Perkins, T.
Starkey, E. A.

C Company. 1917.

Stow, E. T.
Barnes, F. C.
Hallum, E. J.
Lambrick, S. W.
Adams, J.
Banks, W. J.
Bestall, A. H.
Cooper, H.
Rush, W.
Wilson, W. R.
Knight, W. C.
Harbour, I.
Lyall, G.
Salter, A. R.
James, F.
Deville, A.
Duncan, F. W.
Fitt, C.
McGrath, W. E.
Neale, H. C.

Woodward, A. W.
Cheshworth, A.
Exeter, F. E.
Hicks, F. B.
Jarmin, R.
Moore, H. J.
Pearce, G.
Herbert, A. T.
Walder, A.
Williams, S. J.
Kendall, W.
Arthur, R. W. H.
Webb, J.
Hitchcock, F. C.
Guiland, M. A.
Collins, W. T.
Sykes, L.
Stanbrough, E. G.
Evans, E. W. H.

D Company. 1917.

Whibley, A.
Garvey, J.
Wood, A.
Axtens, H. M.
Burnham, S. G.
Dryden, G.
Hawkes, C. W.
Palfrey, W.
Singleton, W.
Waugh, G. W.
Whitchurch, A.
Burge, S. H. O.
Howes, J. W.
Williams, W. F.
Isaac, B.
Marks, J. H.
Rowland, O.
Shock, A. E.
Southcliffe, C. W.
Speakman, J.
Tomlinson, J. E.
Minter, F. S.
Goodhall, C. R.

Mardell, P. W.
Saunders, W.
Richardson, E.
Ward, F. G. A.
Evans, P. J.
Mallett, J. F.
Brown, J.
Crosby, C. T.
Pratt, H. J.
Senior, J. W.
Turner, B. P.
Walton, A. E.
Towndrow, A.
Gallagher, J. A.
Knight, W.
Stevens, C.
Merriott, C. W.
Ramsey, R. C.
Manning, F. J.
Miles, G.
Martin, G. P.
Cursen, F. W.

22nd R.F. Old Comrades Association

(KENSINGTON BATTALION).

Headquarters—156, Ladbroke Grove, W.11.

President :—
Sir Wm. H. Davison, K.B.E., M.P., J.P., D.L.

Vice Presidents :—
His Worship the Mayor of Kensington,
Councillor A. J. Allen, M.A., J.P.

Lieut.-Col. Sir Alan H. Burgoyne, K.B.E., J.P.

Rear-Admiral J. de Courcey Hamilton.

Alderman Sir A. J. Rice-Oxley, C.B.E., J.P., M.D., M.R.C.P.
(Ex-Mayor of Kensington).

COMMITTEE.

Chairman :—
Mr. G. Varley, 11, Stanley Gardens, Kensington Park, W.11.

Vice Chairmen :—
Mr. R. M. Abbott, 67, High Street, Harlesden, N.W.10.
Mr. Ralph Durand, Savage Club.
Mr. J. J. Munro, 2, Durban Road, Beckenham, Kent.

and

Major Christopher Stone, D.S.O., M.C., Pepper's, Ashurst, Steyning,
Mr. P. Basden, 281, Cornwall Road, W.11.   Sussex.
Mr. C. E. Heywood, 64, Chancellors Road, Hammersmith, W.6.
Mr. G. H. Hartley, 68, Waldegrave Road, Teddington.
Mr. F. J. C. Pignon, 77, Herne Hill, S.E.24.
Mr. W. A. Rumble, D.C.M., 20, Mornington Road, N.W.1.
Mr. S. A. Gordon, 5, Vaughan Avenue, Stamford Brook, W.6.
Mr. L. C. McCausland, 40, Dulwich Road, S.E.24.
Mr. E. Phillips, 39, Crofton Road, Peckham, S.E.
Mr. Danvers Ellis, 2 Bourdon Road, Anerley, S.E.
Mr. J. M. Sullivan, 141, Herries Street, W.10.
Mr. E. Griffin, M.M., 66, Richmond Street, W.2.
Mr. C. James, 6, Boscombe Road, Shepherd's Bush, W.12.

Mufti :
Mr. J. M. Greenslade, M.M., 43, Penywern Road, S.W.5.

Hon. Treasurer :—
Mr. W. H. Metcalfe, D.C.M., 11, Greenhill Road, Harrow.

Hon. Sec :—
Mr. R. M. Abbott,
   67, High Street,
      Harlesden, N.W.10.

Asst. Hon. Sec. :—
Mr. H. Rosewarne,
   55, Ledbury Road,
      Bayswater, W.11.